"Coming out of the devastating impacts of COVID-19 on the hotel industry, *Room to Grow* is a must-read for every hotelier who wants to ensure their sales team not only has the right skill set but, even more importantly, the right mindset to thrive."

RACHEL HUMPHREY EVP and COO, AAHOA

"Don't leave sales to chance! *Room to Grow* is filled with tons of rock-solid strategies and practical advice."

JILL KONRATH author of SNAP *Selling* and *More Sales, Less Time*

"*Room to Grow* is a great read! Tammy Gillis provides a balanced combination of valuable high-level strategic advice paired with practical, executable tactics. The timing couldn't be better, given the opportunities (and, of course, challenges) ahead, as we emerge from the pandemic. This book is equally important for GMs, owners, brand leaders, and non-sales hotel team members."

BRIAN LEON president, Choice Hotels Canada

"Required reading for hotel owners, managers, and sales associates!"

IRWIN PRINCE president and COO, Realstar Hospitality

ROOM
TO
GROW

The Sales Handbook
for Hotels

ROOM

═ TO ═

GROW

NOT LEAVING
SALES
TO CHANCE

TAMMY GILLIS

PAGE TWO

Cataloguing in publication information is
available from Library and Archives Canada.
ISBN 978-1-77458-105-6 (paperback)
ISBN 978-1-77458-106-3 (ebook)

Page Two
pagetwo.com

Edited by James Harbeck
Copyedited by Crissy Calhoun
Proofread by Alison Strobel
Cover and interior design by
Setareh Ashrafologhalai

gillissales.com

THIS BOOK IS dedicated to all the incredible hospitality professionals who, despite a devasting year that forever changed our industry, remained resilient, selfless, and dedicated to taking care of guests and employees as they dealt with the biggest crisis we have ever faced. Our industry is made up of extraordinary people who managed to adapt and deliver new standards in hospitality under the toughest of conditions. The road to recovery will not be easy; however, I am full of optimism for brighter days ahead and I am so grateful to be in such great company.

CONTENTS

INTRODUCTION
So Much Room to Grow

MOST PEOPLE DON'T enjoy interacting with sales-people, and yet we're all consumers and we all need to buy.

Salespeople and sales as a profession have a bad rap, and the hospitality industry is no exception. Working in the industry for over 28 years, I've seen sales done poorly more often than I'd like to admit. But it doesn't have to be that way.

This is a book about sales, but not the transactional "rates, dates, and space" kind of sales that has defined us for most of the past decade. No, this is about not leaving sales to chance. This book is about approaching sales with strategic, thoughtful, business-focused action that achieves results during good economic times and, combined with hard work and grit, meets revenue goals when times are tough.

And times have gotten tough. The hospitality industry has faced more than its share of disruption. As we emerge from the challenges of the COVID-19 pandemic, we must push the reset button and take a hard look at our approach to sales and its effectiveness.

Perhaps you are a hotel owner, a director of sales, a general manager, a sales manager, or a student studying hospitality. I know you have the same passion for the industry that I do. It's in our blood (it's not because of the pay or the convenient hours!). Those of us who are attracted to hospitality have a genuine desire to serve and help people. We're driven to bring travelers together, welcome them as our guests, and deliver great customer experiences. And to do that, we need to have the right sales and marketing approach to bring them in.

I wrote this book to elevate hospitality sales—and the work you do—as a critical component in the success of any hotel, brand, or management company. It's time that sales is understood far beyond its practical role. It's time that sales is thought about all the time, not just when bookings decline. Sales needs to be part of the overall business (or commercial) strategy. It shouldn't be a mystery to anyone even indirectly connected to the actual function. The right people need to understand it, support it, and see themselves as part of it.

This book will tell you how to make this happen.

You're going to read about sales fundamentals—the art and science of sales, processes, systems, and tactics that are missing across the industry when salespeople are onboarded and trained. Today's digital tools can help you work smarter and appear more tech savvy, but everyone, from the front desk clerk to the general manager, needs to know enough to be dangerous when it comes to sales.

I also want to shine a light on the industry as a viable, respected career. This means shifting the mindset of how you approach selling to properly set you up for success. This will attract good people back to the industry, increase engagement, and reduce our traditionally high turnover rates.

The perspective I'm going to share in this book is gained from experiences I've been really fortunate to have. I've had an incredible 28-year career in sales (and I'm not retiring anytime soon), and I also share what I've learned from building a sales organization with more than 30 employees and hundreds of clients with a mission to make sales accessible and achievable to all hotel owners. Every day, I personally witness what a difference it makes when an entire organization views sales as a critical part of the overall business strategy and not just a bunch of reactive activities. I see what happens when hotels have the right sales plan in place, with the right people, who are trained and supported to be successful. I celebrate when both sales and operations feel connected to the vision of the entire organization and aren't in their own silos. Even more importantly, I see the results when buyers experience a business conversation with a salesperson who is prepared, shares insights, and offers valuable solutions.

If you have struggled with finding and keeping good salespeople and have had an inconsistent approach to sales, this book is for you. If you are in operations and oversee the sales function, this book is for you. And if you are a director of sales or a sales manager and want to elevate your game so you are more effective and relevant, this book is for you.

This book isn't just about recovering from a pandemic. It's about not leaving sales to chance regardless of the economic environment. There's a lot of work to be done, but there's so much potential.

Or, as I like to put it, so much *room to grow.*

A PERFECT STORM
How Did We Get Here?

*What worked for salespeople the past 10 years
is not going to work for them in the future.
The playing field has been leveled.*

I T WAS the perfect storm.

After a decade of robust growth, the cracks in the North American hospitality industry were beginning to show. Then the COVID-19 pandemic hit, and with it, an economic downturn that had an impact on travel nine times worse than 9/11.[1] Everything came to a grinding halt.

But for anyone looking closely, symptoms had already been showing. The biggest indicator was in RevPAR (revenue per available room) growth. Up until 2019, RevPAR had increased each year for a decade, at about 3 percent a year. However, 2019 was declared the "worst since the recession," dropping from 3 percent to 0.9 percent growth. This drop was nothing compared to what happened when COVID hit, but it was a sign that not everything was right in the industry. Clear vulnerabilities had accumulated during a record period of expansion and growth.

Without a doubt, the COVID pandemic hit the industry hard, but it wasn't the only cause of the challenges facing hotels now trying to build sales in an industry shaken to its core. A storm had already been brewing that exposed what was really going on: leaving sales to chance and not knowing what to do when leads aren't pouring in.

State of sales pre-COVID, 2009–2019

When the economy is good and hotels are making money, it's easy for sales to fly under the radar. It is often not closely inspected or even fully understood by those in operations who oversee it. Before COVID, hotels had some serious cracks in how sales was being executed that the pandemic tore wide open.

Difficulty finding and keeping good salespeople

The hospitality industry is one of the world's largest employers. It also has an extremely high annual turnover rate: 73.8 percent.[2] Sales and operations are no exception. In a good economy, this means a labor shortage for those running sales departments in hotels or trying to make their own sales quotas.

Over the decade before 2020, it had become almost impossible to find and keep a good salesperson. For a few dollars more, your star player in sales could be persuaded to join the competition. Finding a replacement could take months, adding a further burden to the already overworked general manager. This was devasting for the sales function.

As a result, sales was forced to take a back seat to operations. Those employed in sales functions were also frustrated. The day-to-day drag of selling rates, dates, and space; getting pulled into operations; and having to attend too many meetings didn't contribute to positive employee engagement. And so the cycle spiraled downward: salespeople ended up going to the competition or leaving the industry altogether.

If you were a general manager responsible for hiring at a hotel, you weren't just struggling with labor shortages; you also weren't even sure what "good" looked like when it came to sales. Perhaps a candidate has worked 15 years as a director of sales. Does that guarantee they are going to increase revenue and bring in new business?

All of this exposed for many hotels a stop-and-start approach to sales, and the constant hiring and retaining of staff—factors that show up when we talk about how most got into the industry in the first place: by *accident*.

Lack of training and SOPs to ensure salespeople were set up for success

No one grows up saying they want to become a professional salesperson when they get older. Most salespeople stumble into their sales career. If there's a labor shortage, they get reassigned, often from operations, because they were good at working at the front desk or as a coordinator showing some aptitude for building relationships. Most have a good overview of the market and may have even taken online training with their brand. They know all the features of the hotel, can conduct a property site inspection with a potential client, and can even attend a networking event and hand out business cards. But for accidental salespeople, that's usually the extent of their training in the sales arena. There's no training or required certification to be a qualified sales professional that ensures there is mastery across various aspects of the job.

This is not the case for other various disciplines in hospitality. Owners, general managers, and operations managers—typically with business degrees and proven business experience—rely on established business processes, quality standards, and methodologies for meeting performance goals and financial results. Accountants have to be certified to oversee an audit; bookkeepers are thoroughly trained in systems and regulations. Food and beverage staff, including executive chefs, sous chefs, and so on, are taught to follow specific protocols for quality, food cost, health, and safety. In housekeeping, there's rigor and process for the way rooms are cleaned and facilities are maintained. There are standard operating procedures (SOPs) in place for the front desk staff to follow, and formal structures to support the various back office functions.

The requirements to be successful and effective in the above roles, in addition to the systems and processes in place, ensure consistency, quality, and performance. Sales doesn't have any of that. But it didn't seem to be a problem as long as the phones were ringing and leads were coming in.

This brings us to the third problem in the state of sales: any salesperson who came into the industry from 2009 to 2019 didn't have to look too far to find business.

A transactional and reactive sales environment (farming rather than hunting)

A strong economy with many demand generators for hotels meant that for years, most salespeople were kept busy managing existing accounts and dealing with incoming inquiries from various channels; that is, they were *farming*. Bookings came in from walk-ins, incoming inquiries, and third-party channels across many market segments.

The hospitality industry can thank a strong economy that delivered these leads—conventions, entertainment events, endless sports tournaments, corporate travel, leisure travel... Hotels also expected their brand to deliver a certain percentage of reservations, so things were humming along for most of the hotel industry between their brand contribution and incoming inquiries.

The other dependency was on OTAS (online travel agencies) for base business. Some hotels would prefer not to work with OTAS because of the high commissions. But in the absence of a proactive sales strategy and corporate business, OTAS became a major sales channel. If your hotel is fully booked, does it really matter where those bookings came from? (Yes, it does matter. It's a very expensive way to build base business, and you're not building loyalty.) For example, if a hotel is doing $3M in revenue and 30 percent of their revenue is through OTAs at a 20 percent commission, that's $180K in annual fees. However, if the hotel can instead build base business through a more effective sales effort and drive that OTA revenue portion down to 15 percent, that's a $90K savings in commission fees.

Below the surface, a dangerous trend was unfolding: the sales function wasn't being properly managed or supported for a time when sales wouldn't just "happen." During an economic downturn or an increase in competition, such as an oversupply of hotels in your market, those who survive do so because sales is something they have consistently and effectively managed in good times and in bad, so they are not starting from scratch. They have experience *hunting* for new revenue sources. But in 2020, not only did many salespeople not know how to hunt, but also few (if any) had even been trained in sales fundamentals.

It's not that they lacked information and data. Salespeople already had the technology and tools they needed at their disposal, but they were not using the information to better understand the customer. They were not taking the time to do research, and they were not taking the time to understand if they were a fit. On all fronts, it was a reactive environment, and hotel teams became complacent. When the downturn hit, and hit hard, hotels suddenly faced a reimagined sales environment, one where salespeople could no longer hide behind their desks as phones stopped ringing and incoming inquiries became nonexistent.

A reimagined sales environment

Several factors converged to make this perfect storm. Let's start connecting some dots.

In the years following the 2008–2009 recession, the global economy slowly recovered, and travel dollars began to flow again. In order to connect and grow, most companies had budgets to travel and hold offsite meetings and events. As a result, corporate travel managers and meeting planners were setting up events around the world; companies, government agencies, and institutions had budgets to send employees to conventions and training. In some organizations, travel is the largest expense category after payroll. Service sectors such as construction were also booming, and construction crews needed places to stay. In sports, athletes, officials, and spectators traveled to professional and amateur events each year.

With money to reinvest, hotel developers and owners kept building hotels. Big-box brands got bigger with mergers and acquisitions and the creation of sub-brands in every product segment: extended stay, upper scale, full service, select service, and lifestyle brands. Developers were building in secondary and tertiary markets. Not too long ago, the only premium choice hotel in town was a Marriott; then, almost overnight, a Fairfield and Courtyard would open, along with an Embassy Suites and Holiday Inn Express.

In some markets, the majority of new hotels being built were in the select service category. This oversupply forced many hotels to look at sales proactively, in order to protect their business from the newest hotel that just opened in their market. As described in an early 2020 market insight report, "Supply growth has been manageable when you look at the total numbers, but there has been a disproportionate amount of new inventory entering the limited-service marketplace. While demand continues to be healthy in those segments, the jump in supply is going to put more pressure on performance levels."[3] Customers were confused, and hotel owners couldn't be sure that another hotel (or two or three) in their brand family wouldn't show up in their market and draw away their customers.

But the hotels kept being built and travelers kept coming. Until they didn't.

At the same time, the brands and hotels continued to compete with OTAs (which had bigger marketing budgets than all brands combined) and looked for ways to increase their direct bookings.

Rise of the OTAs

By 2016, OTA bookings in the US exceeded total hotel website gross bookings.[4] While OTAs are the subject of much controversy and animosity, they were clearly not going away, and they had become a strong competitor, despite their high commission rates.

The rise of the OTAs created a new role in the hospitality industry: revenue management. The proliferation of online booking channels, and the role of revenue managers and their relationship to operations, made life complicated for those in hospitality sales. Revenue management became its own discipline, separated and in most instances sitting on the opposite side of the table from sales. Armed with data and analytics, revenue managers tried to balance the relationship between how a hotel room is priced and what a consumer pays for that room. There is an inherent conflict between revenue management and sales and how they're evaluated: revenue managers typically want a high rate, while salespeople want to bring in clients at discounted rates who can provide base business throughout the year. And there hasn't been a lot of cross-training or collaboration between these roles.

Regardless of economic conditions, hotel teams could no longer afford to operate in silos this way. Revenue management, operations, sales, and marketing needed to work together—and believe me, in most cases, this was not happening. It was another disconnect that the industry faced after a decade of good times.

Evolution of the modern buyer

According to Daniel Pink, bestselling author of *To Sell Is Human*, sales has changed more in the past 10 years than in the previous 100. Driving the change are technology and the availability of information. Buyers are more informed than ever before and no longer need salespeople for information. As a consequence, salespeople no longer are gatekeepers of information about their product or service.

To sum up today's buyers in three points:

- Digitally driven and mobile empowered
- Socially connected to information and people
- Expect personalization, transparency, and immediate fulfillment (think Amazon)

As 2020 rolled around, customers across all industries were not the same customers from 10 or 20 years ago. They had evolved. Thanks to technology, the world had entered the era of the modern buyer. With the internet at their fingertips, modern buyers search, view, and compare rates, dates, and space. They read online reviews from wherever they are, at any time of the day, and do all these activities quicker than waiting for a salesperson to get back to them. The salesperson, in fact, just got in their way.

As Google's *ZMOT Handbook* for marketers explains, "the sales funnel isn't really a funnel anymore." Or, as described by John Ross of Shopper Sciences, today's buyer journey "looks less like a funnel and more like a flight map."[5]

You would think that this new equal playing field between buyer and seller, in terms of availability of information, would change the approach of the salesperson. It didn't. Technology had made the transactional aspects of sales easier, but it masked the fact that salespeople weren't meeting clients where they were in their buying process, and so they weren't adding value to what buyers could find on their own online.

Today's buyers may be more informed, but they are also overwhelmed with information. They are tired of unprepared salespeople calling them with no idea what their company does and how that seller can help. They quickly lose interest when it's left to them to connect the dots to figure out if and why a hotel is a good fit.

Yet salespeople continued to have *sales* conversations, instead of making use of all of the technology and tools available to have relevant *business* conversations. This approach has consequences—and an impact on a hotel's success. It's not that salespeople haven't embraced technology, including social selling and a dizzying array of digital tactics. But in too many instances, technology has become a tool for doing the same old things faster. At worst, smarter and faster hotel technology has actually made it easier to avoid a face-to-face conversation or a telephone call by instead sending out a mass, impersonal email. But whether a salesperson uses traditional or e-tools, the same problem exists; too many continue to sell like it's 1990, showing up late into the client's buying process and failing to be relevant.

These new realities present an opportunity for those who are willing to make some fundamental shifts in how they approach sales. What do we need to do to elevate sales in the hospitality industry and move forward with a strong sales imperative? Let's start with a sales checkup.

ARE YOU SELLING LIKE IT'S 1990?
A Sales Checkup

"In this world the celebrated 'solution sales rep'
can be more of an annoyance than an asset."
HARVARD BUSINESS REVIEW[1]

O VER THE YEARS, I have trained thousands of directors of sales, operations staff, owners, and general managers. Many fit the description of "accidental" salespeople, others have been in sales most of their career, and the rest are responsible for sales even though it's not in their job description. Every assignment is different; every brand, franchise, single hotel owner, general manager, or team comes with circumstances and resources unique to them. But our clients have one thing in common: they are struggling with sales.

There are many theories about what's causing the problem: the competition, the failure of the brand to adequately support them, the economy, aggressive OTAS, Airbnb, or the pandemic (understandably). Others admit they don't know why they're struggling but are equally frustrated.

Regardless of the reasons, barriers, or even catastrophic circumstances, the symptoms causing the pain are all similar. We've found that by recognizing the symptoms, you can determine the root cause and find a better solution. So, let's do a sales checkup: do you see yourself in any of the following five scenarios?

Mary: Smiling and dialing

Here we have Mary, a conscientious sales manager who is determined to do the work necessary to bring in new leads. She's not afraid of cold calling—in fact, in her interview for the job, she talked about how she cold called in her former job and always found that eventually someone said yes.

Every day, Mary sits down with a list of new prospects and inactive accounts and gets ready for her calls. She has a list of the top employers in the city that she is going to start prospecting. She checks in with herself and says, "Today is going to be a good day for sales." Mary's determined to get a few more leads by the end of the day; then at least she will feel like she's accomplished something. Mary jumps right in and starts calling her list of prospects. After all, she has done this a thousand times before and knows exactly what to say.

But of the 20 calls Mary makes this morning, she only gets to speak with two people. One project manager asks if she could send him some information; they will keep it on hand if anything comes up, but currently they don't have any travel needs. Another says they already have a preferred hotel they use in the city, but they are willing to have rates in place at Mary's hotel in case they need an overflow option. The rest of the calls go to voicemail—and most, of course, will never call back.

When Mary's general manager reviews her progress at the end of the week, he will find that Mary hasn't booked any new business. She's left a lot of voicemail messages, sent emails, and is waiting to hear back from these prospects. The general manager, not understanding sales, doesn't know what to look for in Mary's sales approach to be able to coach and course correct her.

Mary sits down after lunch and begins her calls once again.

 CHECKUP

Is your sales team smiling and dialing without adequate planning, research, and preparation ahead of time—only to wind up frustrated because no one calls them back, or when they do, all the customer wants is a cheaper rate? This is the most common symptom we see. It consumes hundreds of hours of time, with current statistics telling us it takes 18 calls to connect to a single buyer,[2] and in the end, all you're doing is giving the customer information they can likely find out on their own.

No prospect wants a call from a salesperson who isn't prepared and is just going to pitch-slap them. Despite the low pickup rate, salespeople need to be prepared as if a prospect will pick up every time.

Cold calling isn't an effective sales strategy; given the information and tools salespeople have at their disposal, Mary needs a sales process and a framework for researching her prospects before picking up the phone or sending an email, if she wants to increase her call-back rates.

Henry: The revolving door on the sales office

Henry owns two hotels: one is an extended stay, the other a select service hotel. Henry's hotels do fairly well, but both lack corporate business during the week and are busier on the weekends. Henry needs a dedicated salesperson to develop business from the corporate market, so his hotels stay ahead of the competition.

Henry's frustration is in hiring and keeping staff. He's about to hire his third salesperson in two years, and he is not looking forward to it. The first time Henry went through the process, he was enthusiastic about his new hire. The young woman seemed perfect for the job. She was friendly and outgoing, and she'd completed a certificate program in hospitality and tourism management. She said she was eager to build a career in the industry. But after six months, she left. Her reason? She accepted a job with one of his competitors for a few more thousand dollars a year.

The next hire stayed longer. He had a lot of sales experience, so Henry left him on his own. When he asked for the latest sales tools, Henry bought them, expecting that it would provide another source of leads for his salesperson. Problem was, the salesperson never left the office to go on sales calls; instead, he just kept waiting for the phone to ring. He preferred keeping busy with incoming inquiries and sending sales emails rather than getting out of the office to find new business.

Now ready to hire his third salesperson, Henry throws up his hands in despair and declares, "I don't even know what 'good' looks like anymore!"

CHECKUP

High turnover and not having the right person in the right seat are disruptive to your business in many ways. It's expensive to continually hire, train, and ramp up a new person only to have them not work out—and then you have to do it all again. Hotels lose momentum and struggle getting traction with their sales efforts. How many salespeople have you hired in the past few years? When you do hire, are you sure what "good" looks like? Are you clear about the characteristics, skills, and mindset you are looking for in a salesperson?

Sales has changed dramatically in the past few years. Sellers need more than just strong product knowledge and interpersonal skills. General managers like Henry have to know how to choose the right salesperson for the right role. Each role profile requires its own skill set and mindset.

Keeping good staff is also a challenge because sales isn't a career most people choose.

Jack: "If I build it, they will come"

Jack remembers the first day he walked across the parking lot as new owner of his beautiful 80-room hotel. The sign on top of the building could be seen from the highway overpass. For Jack, having a Marriott-branded hotel was the beginning of a great future. He'd struggled in previous businesses, running smaller, independent hotels that didn't have any brand presence. It seemed he was always losing customers to the big brands. "I like your hotel," they'd say, "but you don't have a loyalty program."

Now everything was going to be different. Jack made the decision not to hire a sales manager. After all, that's why he chose a hotel with a recognized brand name. With only 80 rooms, he should be able to do 65–70 percent occupancy, considering incoming leads, the brand's reservation system, and third-party channels. Or at least, that's what he assumes.

But within a year, two new big-box brands have opened a few miles away, also with signs that can be seen from the highway. Both are select service. To Jack's dismay, one is even a Marriott! Over the next few months, he notices revenue is pacing behind last year, but he can't point to the exact reason why. He wears so many hats as an owner and operator; how is he going to add sales to his job description?

 **CHECKUP**

Jack had expected his hotel sign alone would bring in business. This is another common misconception. In a thriving economy, there's enough demand generators to send Jack and his competitors all the bookings they need. But in a tough economy or when there's oversupply in the market and not enough business to go around, the brand alone isn't enough.

The truth is that even during a thriving economy, a "build it and they will come" mentality isn't sustainable. A successful hotel needs a strong local sales strategy and presence in the market. No brand will deliver enough business to keep a hotel busy all year round, and brands are not going to take care of a hotel's backyard sales.

Jill: The farmer who has to hunt

Last year, Jill was named one of the top salespersons of the year from her management group. It was a busy year but very satisfying. She was responsible for all market segments and had a junior sales coordinator that helped her with some of the administrative work. Her days were filled with keeping up with incoming inquiries, meeting clients over lunch, and working with her favorite corporate travel managers and event planners to negotiate contracts for their hotel programs, meetings, and conventions. Jill had no reason to expect that next year's bookings would be any different. In fact, she already had an impressive number of room nights on the books for the next 12 months.

Then everything changed. In the spring of 2020, travel came to an almost total standstill, and so did the hospitality industry. Jill's time was spent fielding calls from clients who had to cancel their bookings. In May, she realized that all of their top clients were no longer traveling; she had to pivot and find other revenue sources for the hotel.

Now Jill just stares at the computer screen in front of her, wondering what to do. She knew how to take care of all those long-term clients in the corporate and convention segment, but she is now being asked to find new business that perhaps the hotel had ignored when times were good. She is overwhelmed and doesn't know where to start.

 CHECKUP

When checking symptoms, we always look for signs of hunting versus farming. There's a big difference between managing inquiries that are coming into your hotel from various sources and hunting for business, and they require a different skill set and mindset. If a salesperson has never sold in an environment of scarcity, they may struggle to pivot. You'll read a lot more about hunting and farming in later chapters.

Ari: Losing opportunities at the front desk

Ari is the general manager of a full-service hotel and conference center. When he has a moment, Ari likes to visit the lobby when travelers arrive to ensure everything is going smoothly at the front desk and to greet guests checking in. Tonight, the lobby is bustling with people. As usual, the front desk staff are working very hard to check people in and direct everyone to where they need to be. But Ari can't help but notice that almost no one at the front desk takes a moment to lift their head and smile, let alone say, "What brings you to town?" or "What company are you with?" They continue to check people in without capturing critical information about them to identify future business opportunities.

Ari knows from the arrivals report that a large percentage of the reservations don't have a corporate name attached to them, especially if they booked on a third-party channel.

 CHECKUP

Are your front desk staff qualifying leads or letting them get away? Do they see themselves as an important part of the sales team or do they see their role as "I check people in, and I check people out"? Do they have the tools, and have they been trained on how to qualify guests at check-in and how to convert incoming inquiries into reservations?

Don't leave it open to interpretation. What gets measured gets done, and it's critical to have SOPs that all front desk staff are trained in for handling check-ins and reservations. They can be an important part of your sales strategy to identify leads and give them to the sales department or general manager for follow-up.

Making a diagnosis

If you can see yourself in any of these stories, you are likely experiencing some pain as it relates to your sales strategy. These stories may be slightly exaggerated (or perhaps not), but they are here to help you recognize the common symptoms in the state of sales in the hospitality industry and to understand how much needs to change.

Each of these symptoms relates back to an overall approach to the sales function that is transactional, not strategic. As a result, in most instances, the fictional people you've just read about are reactive, not proactive. There's an immediate problem, so they solve it. There's competition, so they offer a better price.

The consequences of these examples take us to the heart of the problem: a lack of sales imperative. In good times, you may get by as a Henry or a Mary; or, like Ari or Jill, you can see there is a problem, but with business coming in the door, operations takes priority over sales. All of this changes during times of scarcity. That's when there's not enough business for everyone, and sales drop dramatically. The numbers back this up: according to a study by CSO Insights pre-COVID, only 53 percent of salespeople were meeting or exceeding their sales targets. The study suggested that sales organizations were not evolving fast enough to meet the needs of today's informed buyers.[3]

It becomes obvious that many hotels have not been in control of their own destiny. They haven't been in the driver's seat. They've been a passenger, happily riding along and taking business as it comes—until it doesn't. This brings us to the first fundamental that has to change: *mindset*.

BECOMING A
MODERN SELLER
Business Conversations
vs. Sales Conversations

*Prospects are not buying what you are
selling. They are buying what your
product or service enables them to do or be.*

WAS ONE OF those accidental salespeople we talked about in chapter 1. Growing up I wanted to be a social worker or in some line of work where I could help people. But after completing a co-op in high school at a women's crisis shelter, I decided this was something I could do on a volunteer basis; it was simply too heart-wrenching as a career.

So off to college I went, where I pursued a three-year program in hospitality and event management. I wanted to be a meeting planner, or so I thought. However, the first job I interviewed for was a corporate sales manager with Hilton Hotels. And I got the job! I couldn't believe it. I was excited, but I thought to myself, "What does a corporate sales manager even do?"

I had become an accidental salesperson.

There was another challenge ahead of me. I had started my sales career in a market with a massive over-supply of hotels and during an economic recession (it was 1993). In hindsight, it was the *best* thing that could have happened to me. It meant that leads weren't coming in the door and the phone wasn't ringing off the hook. (Phones rang back in the 1990s!)

Being in sales during a recession and competing with the dozens and dozens of hotels in and around the Toronto airport gave me no choice: I had to learn how to find *new* business. I had to learn to hunt for business—and to be good at it. Being good at it meant not sounding like every other salesperson who was trying to get the customer's business. It meant looking at the sales process from the customer's perspective.

This didn't happen overnight. Like most salespeople, I was thrown into the deep end, shown my desk, given a tour of the hotel and a territory to manage. I started out having sales conversations, not business conversations. But over time and through trial and error, I got better and became a more relevant seller.

Sales conversations

Sales conversations are focused on the product or the service the vendor is selling, with little thought as to how it might help the buyer. The buyer is left to connect the dots and figure out if it's a good fit. The seller does more talking—and less listening to understand the prospect's values and pain points. It's a very generic and transactional approach to business development.

Think about how salespeople are trained and onboarded when they start at a new hotel. They are trained ad nauseam on the features of the hotel, given a tour of the property, lunch in the restaurant, a sales kit, and then expected to determine what differentiates them from their competitive set for the various customer types they are going to prospect. It's left up to their interpretation, assuming the trained salesperson will know what to say and do. Very little time is spent talking about business strategy or understanding various market segments and industries to evaluate what their travelers might care about. Salespeople are hardwired to be experts about their product... when they need to become experts about their customers and their buying process.

Selling from a customer's perspective is not a new idea. In 1936, Dale Carnegie made it one of the main points in his famous work, *How to Win Friends and Influence People*. Carnegie wrote, "Try honestly to see things from the other person's point of view."[1] He suggested this was the most important principle in the entire book. Salespeople ever since have instructed their teams to do the same: "Walk in the other person's shoes," "assess the customer's needs," "find a solution by looking at the situation through the customer's lens."

So, the million-dollar question remains: Why, despite the availability of information, technology, and data, do salespeople continue to show up unprepared to customer meetings or prospecting calls and default to conversations that are all about them? ("Let me tell you more about our 300 beautifully appointed rooms...") What makes them continue to approach the corporate customer with the same sales pitch as they use on the sports coach or the construction contractor, when their needs and values are so different? It's not necessarily a lack of sales skills or experience, because we see this happen even with the most experienced sellers.

It turns out we all like to talk about ourselves. An article by Adrian F. Ward in *Scientific American* titled "The Neuroscience of Everybody's Favorite Topic"[2] notes that people spend about 60 percent of conversations talking about themselves. The study is backed up with research on how the human brain works. It turns out that "me-focused" conversations activate the same area of the brain that lights up when eating good food, taking drugs, and even having sex. It feels good to talk about ourselves, so of course that's what we do!

Salespeople are no exception. In one study, 25,537 business-to-business (B2B) sales conversations were recorded and analyzed. Findings showed that the average B2B sales rep spent between 65 and 75 percent of a call talking, leaving only 25 to 35 percent of the call for listening. It doesn't take a big change to improve the results. The same study showed that increasing the chance for the prospect to talk from 22 percent to 33 percent significantly increased opportunity win rates.[3]

Making a conversation "all about you" leads to another problem. When salespeople fail to listen and fail to ask the right questions, they actually believe they are looking at a situation from another person's point of view. This is not the case. They are simply assuming the customer's point of view from their own set of assumptions.

Business conversations

Business conversations shift the focus from the vendor's product or service to how the product or service enables the customer. It's a very subtle shift in perspective but has major implications on the buying experience and therefore the success rate of a seller.

A typical prospecting call goes like this:

> Hi, I'm Tammy. I'm calling from ABC Hotel in Chicago. We are a newly renovated full-service hotel located 10 minutes from the airport. I'm calling to inquire if you have any hotel needs in our area and, if so, I would like to discuss setting up a corporate rate for your travelers.

There are a few reasons this typical sales pitch doesn't work and isn't appreciated by anyone:

1   The seller has done very little research and is putting the responsibility on the prospect to educate the seller on their needs. This seller will be the easiest person to shut down and not get past hello.

2   They immediately start selling their newly renovated hotel near the airport. That means nothing if

you haven't done your research to know whether that matters to the buyer.

3   This approach benefits the seller and adds no value to the buyer.

With a little bit of research, the right shift in mindset to understand what this prospect might need or care about will help sellers rise above the noise, stand out, and have a shot at getting a prospect to listen. Here is an example of a prospecting call that is a business conversation rather than a sales conversation:

> Hi, I'm Tammy Gillis and I'm calling from the ABC Hotel in Chicago. I was speaking with John Smith, your VP of finance, who is a regular guest at our hotel, and he recommended we connect. I understand you are looking at bringing your leadership team to Chicago for a meeting next quarter, and I'd love to better understand your needs and see how we help you with this important event.

Now, instead of a transactional conversation, you are having a business conversation. Notice the shift in mindset. In this example, the seller mentions that John Smith recommended they connect, so this is no longer a cold call. The caller has taken the time to find out what the customer is looking for (that is, truly looked at the situation from the customer's perspective). Instead of making assumptions, the salesperson is able to refer to the specific way in which the hotel can meet an upcoming need.

Do you understand what your customers are buying?

Listening in order to gain customer perspective is only part of what you need to do. Today's hospitality salespeople and those who support them have to be able to distinguish between what they are selling and what their customer is buying. This is different for every customer. A generic sales approach will only make you sound like every other salesperson who has called before. This isn't a skill set; it's a mindset.

To illustrate the disconnect that typically happens, take a moment to consider the following three customer scenarios:

1 A corporate customer is bringing in a large group of new hires for a two-day training event.

2 A contractor has a crew in town for seven days, including the weekend, for a new construction project in the area.

3 A sports coach is bringing in a team of young athletes competing in the area for a tournament.

Next, answer the question: What are you selling? (Check all that apply.)

☐ Lovely rooms at a recognized hotel in the area

☐ The best loyalty program

☐ A hot breakfast, free Wi-Fi, free parking, and mobile check-in

- ☐ Great services and great value

- ☐ The newest hotel in town with a restaurant and an indoor swimming pool

- ☐ An extended-stay hotel with kitchenettes and laundry facilities

All of the above features could apply to any of the three customers (some more than others). The same features could be offered by the competition. This information can be found (and compared) online; the customer doesn't even need you to provide this information. So, if this is what you are selling, there is no compelling reason why any of these customers are going to select you over someone else—unless, of course, they can get a lower rate.

You need to put more "meat on the bones" and understand what the customer is really buying. Otherwise, all you do is feature dump, blend in with every other hotel, and force customers to make a decision on price because you haven't given them anything else to go on.

To have a business conversation, you need to understand what each customer values and what a typical day in the life looks like for these customers. You can then speak their language, ask relevant questions, and provide very specific solutions that communicates to the buyer that you are listening, and you are not going to waste their time with a sales pitch.

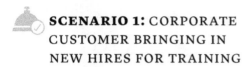

SCENARIO 1: CORPORATE CUSTOMER BRINGING IN NEW HIRES FOR TRAINING

This company is bringing in a large group of new hires for its annual training event. The company has established a reputation for its excellent onboarding experience, so making a positive first impression is key. With most travelers arriving from across the country, they want a hotel that is close to the airport and offers shuttle service. In light of recent concerns about health and safety, they are looking for a place for travelers to stay that is safe, clean, and close to their corporate office where training sessions are being held. Wi-Fi, a business center, and a restaurant that offers a hot breakfast to start their day are important. They expect the hotel to extend their preferred corporate rate to this group for the week and to provide welcome cards and a small treat basket in each of the rooms.

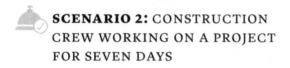

SCENARIO 2: CONSTRUCTION CREW WORKING ON A PROJECT FOR SEVEN DAYS

The contractor needs accommodation for seven days straight and is looking for a hotel close to the construction site with a well-lit, big parking lot so their trucks are safe overnight. The crew needs laundry service and flexible housekeeping hours. Crews typically need to be on the construction site by 7 a.m., so a full breakfast needs to be available starting at 5:30 a.m. Information on nearby restaurants would be appreciated. They also need a hotel that offers a rate within their per diem.

SCENARIO 3: SPORTS COACH
RESPONSIBLE FOR A TEAM
OF YOUNG ATHLETES

The sports coach and team managers are responsible for a group of young adults, trainers, and adult chaperones. Athletes need to be accommodated close to the competition facility, with room in the parking lot to accommodate the team bus. The team needs to be on one floor, if possible, with access to the fitness facilities and a room for the group to meet in the evening. Managers would like to have input into what is served at breakfast to ensure players start the day with enough protein. They need box lunches because they stay at the arena most of the day. As an amateur sports team, they are funded through fees and donations, so a budget-friendly rate is expected, along with rooms with two beds.

Imagine you approached each of these customers with the same sales pitch when their needs and reasons for traveling are so different. What message would you be sending to them? Remember, customers are not buying what you are selling—they are buying a solution that fulfills their needs and reasons for traveling. Staying at a hotel is a means to an end. It's up to salespeople to understand why they are traveling in the first place.

What are the implications if salespeople don't make this shift? According to a 2018 CSO Insights study titled *The Growing Buyer-Seller Gap*,[4] buyers are evolving faster than sales organizations.

And the implications are real:

- Sellers get engaged later in the sales process.

- Sellers are unable to clarify needs, shape solutions, and provide valuable recommendations.

- It becomes a transactional conversation about price and contract details.

- Buyers see no differentiation between sellers; they all sound the same.

Customers are consumers first and they bring their expectations of personalization, transparency, and immediate fulfillment to their work environments.

How would you rank if your top customers were to define your relationship? What category would they put you in?

Approved vendor: Buyer believes the seller has acceptable product/service. Seller is one of several companies the customer can buy from.

Preferred supplier: Seller is seen as having a successful track record and has an expanded number of contacts in the company.

Solutions consultant: Focus is on the customer's business challenges and issues and on offering solutions.

Trusted partner: Seller is recognized as an expert in the industry and an added value to buyers. Seller is invited to participate in internal meetings held by buyer.

This is a good benchmark to better understand how vulnerable your client relationships are to competitors and where you need to invest some time and energy to protect your business.

Why the sales role needs to evolve

To meet buyers where they are in their buying process and to encourage them to engage with you earlier so you can ask discovery questions and help shape their solutions, we have some work to do. For the most part, our sales profession is still selling in a traditional, transactional way. Let's look at how traditional sales needs to evolve into modern selling to avoid extinction.

Traditional Selling Skills	Modern Selling Skills
Sales acumen focused on: <ul><li>Product knowledge</li><li>Interpersonal skills</li><li>Sales pitches/presentations</li><li>Selling skills (always be closing)</li><li>Systems and reporting</li></ul>	Business acumen focused on: <ul><li>Knowledge of clients and their industry</li><li>Market industry trends</li><li>Sales, marketing, and social media</li><li>Revenue management</li><li>Exceptional communication skills</li><li>Relevant and well-crafted value propositions</li><li>Repeatable sales process and systems</li><li>Problem solver and consultant</li><li>Analysis of data and performance</li></ul>

I guarantee that once you start looking at sales through the lens of your clients, you'll see an increase in engagement and results. But it's not going to happen without revisiting some business and sales fundamentals that may be common sense but are not common practice. Let's dive in.

STRATEGY BEFORE TACTICS
Building Your Business Plan

Strategy and tactics are often used interchangeably as if they were synonyms when, in fact, they are very different things.

WHEN I WAS 28, I was director of sales at a large full-service hotel that had 30,000 square feet of meeting space and was connected to a convention center. I had 10 direct reports and oversaw both the sales and catering departments. In addition to overseeing the sales and marketing strategy for the hotel, I was actively selling. I was responsible for a couple of market segments, so like most directors of sales, I was toggling back and forth between being in the clouds strategic planning and being in the weeds executing the strategy with our team.

We did amazing things together in a difficult market. Within two years, our hotel went from last in our comp set to second. It was an insane amount of work, and I learned the hard way why it's so easy for strategy to get pushed aside in favor of all the busy "doing" that can take over your day.

Strategic planning took time and it needed space away from the office. As a director of sales, I was part of the business planning process, together with our general manager, our front office manager, and our controller. I learned so much from this process and the value of having input from all key departments.

What is strategy, and why do salespeople default to tactics?

Strategy and tactics are often used interchangeably as if they were synonyms when, in fact, they are very different things. It's not just semantics.

Strategy is the *what*: the overarching plan or set of objectives.

Tactics are the *how*: the specific actions or steps you execute to accomplish your strategy.

If you don't take the time to figure out the what (strategy), then you likely aren't executing the right how (tactics).

So why do salespeople go straight to the tactics? Part of the problem is the environment I described above, where operations and day-to-day activities interfere with (or override) the planning process. The hotel environment doesn't set you up with the time to do the critical thinking necessary to formulate a business strategy and subsequent sales plan.

Smaller hotels rarely create a formal strategic business plan. Larger hotels and management companies do, but once the planning is complete, the focus shifts back to operations, rather than taking time to evaluate the results of the plan, see what's working and what's not based on market conditions, and adjust along the way.

Another reason relates to how people process information. There are over 150 cognitive biases that affect the way individuals think about and see the world. The availability bias, for instance, affects thinking processes such as decision-making and planning. It supports the theory that people are tactical, not strategic in nature—that is, wired to fill an immediate need (such as "I want an ice cream cone") rather than to satisfy a long-term goal ("I want to lose weight"). It's the same bias that gives us a tendency to place more weight on information that comes to mind easily than on other objectives or more important facts.[1]

In short, our default setting is to be busy bees, rather than taking a step back and figuring out the what and the why of our business strategies.

What to include in your business plan

Franchising.com defines the business planning process as "knowing where you want to go and how to get there to end up in the right place." I am not a fan of an annual business planning process because business is fluid and it's difficult to forecast revenue and expenses 12 months in advance. I do understand this might not work for all businesses and that owners and management companies may require a traditional business planning process for their lenders, owners, and leadership teams. Our company works two quarters in advance, which allows us to get more granular and make better decisions about our revenue and expenses without trying to predict a year in advance.

Strategic objectives

Start with the what. For example:

- Increase our competitive position in the market from fourth to second place in comp set

- Reduce our reliance on OTAs and increase our mix of corporate business by 15 percent

- Attract additional higher-rated leisure business on weekends

- Shift our weekday market mix from low-rated crew business to higher-rated corporate business

Economic and industry outlook

The next step is to look ahead at the next 12 to 18 months.

If the economy changes, the demand generators will change as well. The most recent example would be the COVID pandemic, where leisure, groups, and corporate travel almost disappeared. No one can predict exactly what's ahead, but you need to do projections based on whether the economy is robust or slowing down and what's driving it in your specific market. Review historical data and industry outlook reports.

Market analysis

What are the major demand generators driving the economy in your market? Are you in a leisure destination that is expecting a banner year with tourists? Is your city a convention destination that will be host to some big events in the coming year? Are you home to sporting facilities that attract national competitions? Or perhaps you are in an industrial market that attracts corporate business?

By understanding your market and what's driving the economy, you will have a good sense of what business market segments to target for both weekday and weekend business.

SWOT analysis

Do a SWOT (strengths, weaknesses, opportunities, threats) analysis of your competitive set and update it throughout the year. This is critical to help you and your team compete in your local market. It will give you a competitive advantage and allow you to:

- Uncover opportunities
- Proactively manage and eliminate threats
- Distinguish yourself from competitors

Consider these questions as you complete your SWOT analysis:

Strengths: What are we good at? What is working in our favor?

Weaknesses: What could we do better?

Opportunities: What external factors could benefit our business? (e.g., new sporting complex to attract national events)

Threats: What external factors could negatively impact our business? (e.g., new hotel in market)

When completing your SWOT, I recommend doing one by market segment for each of your competitors. Without an understanding of who you compete with and why, by segment, you are not able to identify your true differentiators, which is critical in overcoming objections and closing the sale. For example, you may uncover that for the sports market, you have more double doubles than XYZ Hotel and that you are the closest hotel to the sports complex. That wouldn't be uncovered if you lumped all segments together under the SWOT.

Many of you may recognize the acronym SMERF, which stands for social, military, educational, religious, and fraternal groups. SMERF is a catch-all bucket that lumps multiple market segments into one category. The term has been used (and overused!) for years in the hospitality industry to represent these smaller market segments as if they're uniform. The fact that this term is still used shows how easy it is to go along with a certain way of thinking, without realizing the flaws in its logic.

Even though all five segments relate to group business, each segment's decision-makers have different needs, along with different buying cycles and decision-making criteria.

Vanilla is a flavor of ice cream. Not a sales strategy.

Pricing strategy

Determining the pricing strategy for your hotel is both an art and a science, and all members of the hotel executive team should be involved in this strategic exercise. There are many factors to consider as you build your revenue forecast:

- Room types
- Value of services offered
- Historical data and past performance
- Business mix
- Supply and demand in the local market
- Pricing in the competitive set
- Market seasonality

Marketing strategy

Next, map out your marketing strategy:

- Value proposition by customer segment
- Marketing plan by channel (digital, print, web)
- Social media plan

- Reputation management (online reviews, guest satisfaction surveys)
- Sales plan by market segment (the *how*)

Get granular on your tactics in your sales plan by market segment, aligning them to the above strategic objectives (e.g., target top 25 corporate accounts staying at comp set using Agency360 and parking lot leads).

Now you are in the driver's seat

Remember the sales checkup you did in chapter 2? We know that salespeople spend a lot of time running around making calls, sending emails, smiling and dialing—and most of them lack a good foundation in the fundamental principles of selling. They're focused on making phone calls to put heads in beds, not on building a sustainable sales pipeline. The result is a lot of busywork and most of it is not aligned with what the hotel needs or what the customer wants.

This is going to change once you have a business plan in place. Your hotel can't be everything to every customer, and resources are limited.

Now that you know what buyers are looking for in a salesperson and what is required to evolve into a modern seller, we are ready to revisit some important fundamentals that have gotten lost along the way.

THE SALES REALITY
The Art and
Science of Selling

*"If you do not have a defined process that moves
your people forward so they can achieve
greater results, then what is it you are managing?"*

KEITH ROSEN[1]

L ET US FOR a moment put ourselves back in the path of
the perfect storm described in chapter 1.

For over a decade, the hospitality industry had
enjoyed leads coming through the sales office, the front
desk, and brand or third-party channels. These are prospects that have a need and already have an interest in
your hotel. The booking window keeps getting shorter
for hotels, and when an inquiry comes in and is successfully handled, it can help your occupancy in the next 30,
60, or 90 days. Having the right people handling these
inquiries who are trained and have the tools to guide

the customer through the sales process is critical to increase your conversion rate. When you are looking at your seven-day forecast and want to increase your business on the books, you may decide to lower your online rates, run a promotion with an OTA, or participate in a brand promotion; as a result, you may see an immediate impact on your occupancy within 24 to 72 hours. These sales and revenue tactics can produce some short-term results and instant gratification.

Meanwhile, when it comes to business development and prospecting, nobody is waiting for a salesperson to call. In fact, the call is an unexpected interruption; given how buyers feel about salespeople, they will be looking for the first chance to get off the phone. This is a very different sales cycle from handling a warm lead coming into the hotel or adjusting rates online or running a promotion on an OTA. Outbound sales and prospecting is a grind and there is no instant gratification. It could take months before you see actual results in terms of booked revenue.

Unfortunately, owners and operators have become accustomed to the instant gratification they've experienced with converting incoming inquiries and managing their online rate strategy and expect to see similar results with an outbound sales strategy.

We see it all the time with hotel owners and operators who hire on-property sellers or third-party companies like ours to do sales for them. They admit they have been leaving sales to chance for too long and should have hired us a year or two ago. When they come to us, they are really struggling with sales and have a sense of urgency to see immediate results. They expect that we are going to be able to find business in that month for the month. I often joke and say to them, "If we had that power, we would be charging a lot more for it." The challenge is that the buying process for prospects doesn't adjust for the fact that a hotel should have started to prospect and fill their sales funnel two years ago.

Realities for today's modern sellers

To use a golf metaphor, incoming inquiries help a hotel's short game, and an outbound sales strategy helps the long game. It's important for hotels to have both. The long game is usually sacrificed because of turnover in the sales department, lack of understanding of the sales process, a higher priority placed on operations, or the choice to take a reactive sales approach.

This is the *first sales reality* for today's sellers to keep in mind when you are prospecting: it's a marathon, not a sprint. You are dealing with people who may not have a need, may not be the decision-maker, or may be happy with their current hotel provider. The largest account I won when I was a director of sales took me two years to land.

Given the state of the industry and today's buyers, it can take up to 12 points of interaction with a prospect to close the business. I've read stats over the years that 90 percent of salespeople stop at three or four attempts. Every interaction needs to be purposeful and have an objective, so you are not just leaving multiple voicemail messages and annoying them 12 different ways. Imagine the opportunity sellers have to capture more business if they keep going, knowing most salespeople tap out.

The *second reality* is that salespeople are going to hear a lot of "no" before they hear "yes." This is a challenge for sellers who don't deal well with rejection and are easily discouraged. If you can understand and accept these realities, then you won't take it personally and you will realize that for every "no" you hear, you are that much closer to hearing a "yes."

Which brings me to my *third reality*: sales is a bit of a numbers game (the science part of the process). I am by no means saying that sales is about quantity over quality. I have always believed—and it's part of our own practice and culture at our company—that it's very much quality over quantity. This is why sales is both an art and a science. You need to execute quality calls and be prepared for every potential interaction, and you need to make a certain number of calls to get enough qualified leads in the sales funnel.

The numbers are not in our favor. According to a study by HubSpot:[2]

- It takes 18 dials to connect to a single buyer.

- Call-back rates are less than 1 percent.

- Less than 24 percent of sales emails are opened.

- Sellers are four times more likely to get a response with a personal connection.

- Half of buyers choose the vendor that responds first.

And don't forget about your existing clients. When hotel owners and general managers hire us to help them with their sales efforts, we often hear, "I only want you going after new business. We have a good handle on our existing clients."

After we conduct our sales assessment, we often discover that their existing clients are also staying with their competitors and the hotel is only getting a small portion of the market share. We also discover that a lot of these key clients haven't been nurtured and the hotel doesn't have a proactive outreach strategy to protect and grow these accounts. Just because you are getting room nights from a client, that does not mean they are loyal and exclusive. There are likely multiple contacts within an organization who book travel that you can develop a relationship with.

Now that you understand these realities, it's important to understand the sales cycle and various stages of the sales process.

The length of the sales cycle varies depending on the market segment you are targeting and where the prospect is at in their buying process. To be successful in finding business in the short, medium, and long term, it's critical that the sales funnel is robust with opportunities at all stages of the sales cycle to increase your sales success. For example, if you are looking for short-term business, you may target construction projects, local corporate accounts, or sports groups. If you are looking to secure larger groups or business from global or national accounts, you need to be working further out, because they have a longer buying cycle and this will impact your medium- to long-term business goals.

This graphic shows the high-level steps in the sales process that a hotel needs to manage to achieve actual revenue and demonstrates why a stop-and-start approach doesn't work.

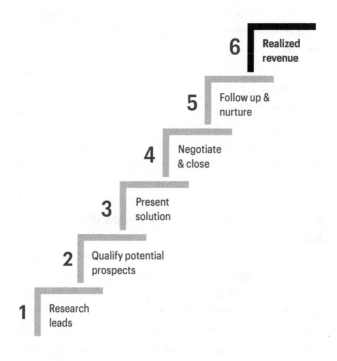

What do these sales realities mean for today's seller?

This longer, more complex sales cycle has various implications for the modern seller. For instance, not every salesperson is going to be great at every stage of the sales process. Some salespeople are great relationship builders but not good at qualifying; others are good at closing, or research, or negotiating. It's rare to find all these strengths in one package.

If you are the sole salesperson managing all segments and all stages of the sales cycle, it's going to be a challenge. You have to play to your strengths and know your blind spots. (This is where training is going to help.) If you are a director of sales or manage a sales team, you want to make sure you have the right person working on the right segments.

Don't take a farmer who's great at converting incoming inquiries or building relationships and put them in the role of a hunter. And, conversely, don't tether a hunter to a desk doing paperwork and managing incoming inquiries when what motivates them is to find and win new business. That will be a slow death for all involved and won't lead to the results required from these roles. Getting the right person in the right seat is critical for successfully executing your sales plan. (We will discuss this more in chapter 7.)

The art and science of selling

Sales is both an art and science, and successful salespeople are proficient at both. The scientific part of sales requires discipline in the execution of repeatable sales strategies that over time lead to success—whether it's prospecting, managing sales opportunities, knowing that sales is a numbers game, or setting revenue goals for the quarter.

It's also an art because high-performing salespeople are great communicators, empathic, have high EQ, and are great relationship builders. They have the grit and resiliency to know the numbers aren't on their side and that they are going to hear "no" a lot more than "yes"—and yet they still persevere.

Managing your pipeline and using a CRM system

To manage its sales activities and pipeline effectively, every hotel, regardless of size, will benefit from a customer relationship management (CRM) system. CRM is a technology for managing all your company's relationships and interactions with customers and potential customers. It consolidates all the data being collected on potential leads and tracks all interactions.

A CRM system *becomes* your sales funnel. It is also the only way a sales director or general manager can do the analytics necessary to inspect and monitor progress, identify stalled leads, and help the sales team focus on activities that generate the most revenue.

Larger hotels have CRM systems like Delphi or Salesforce, but most select service hotels still manage the process manually. If you want to build a sales-focused culture and not leave sales to chance, managing a sales function on spreadsheets or sticky notes is not effective, and you will no doubt miss out on revenue opportunities that are not being properly managed. It's also a risky practice because if a salesperson leaves, they take all of the information with them and the hotel has to start from scratch.

Research possible lead sources

With a CRM system to manage your pipeline, you are now ready to start collecting those qualified leads.

The objective is to find as many leads as possible that can turn into qualified opportunities. Where are you going to find these leads? How do you determine if they have travel needs?

For each market segment you want to develop business from, you need to identify various lead sources. For construction, for example, a lead source could be an online paid subscription service such as BidClerk; for corporate, it could be getting a list of the top 50 companies in your area.

Other lead sources:

- Brand reports (travel agency, daily arrivals, corporate production)

- Qualifying guests at check-in

- Parking lot checks

- Existing clients

- Sports facilities

- Fishbowl at the front desk to capture business cards

- Partnerships with festivals, banquet halls, funeral homes, golf courses

- Lost business/inactive accounts

- Google Alerts

- Convention visitors' bureau or tourism office

- Chamber of commerce

Finding the right or additional decision-makers

Once you've identified your lead sources, you want to identify at least one decision-maker, so you have a direct contact. In a recent poll we conducted, 47 percent of respondents indicated that finding the right decision-maker was their greatest challenge when it came to sales. The problem has been made worse by the fact that so many executives are now working offsite and screening their calls to avoid being solicited by a salesperson.

Start with the company website and LinkedIn page.

- Do they have an org chart? Do they list their executive team?

- Review their newsletters, press releases, and blogs for tips about new projects, new senior hires, and any kind of information that opens up a possibility.

- Think of yourself as an investigative reporter during this stage of the process. It's going to take a lot of grit and tenacity to track down every bit of information you can to find something useful. The deeper you dig into what you can find out about the company, the greater the likelihood that you will identify various potential decision-makers and what areas of their business may require travel.

- Don't forget your existing clients. Are there other decision-makers within the company you can get introduced to who may benefit from working with you?

You're following the breadcrumbs and you'll be amazed at what you learn—not just what you get once you find a few names, but how much you pick up along the way that you can use during your sales call. Even if you've purchased a lead subscription service for finding decision-makers, you'll still need to do this research. A contact list may provide names, but you need to figure out the why before you pick up the phone and call them: Why should they listen to you? Why should they leave their current hotel they are happy with? Why are you better?

Researching the company

The way you identify leads and decision-makers and build relationships is going to be a mix of fundamentals that worked 20 years ago and modern tools and technology. It's not about one or the other; it's about pairing the two to elevate your approach as a relevant seller. For example, you may meet a potential lead at a networking event or trade show, but you'll use social media to learn more about the person and their company before setting up your first call. Perhaps you'll set up a Google Alert to keep current on the company's activities.

Numerous tips and tactics can be used to help with research. Again, this is where a combination of online and traditional tools is going to help.

Look for vendors and partners. When you're researching a company in your area, find out what companies they partner with, either by checking their website or by researching through shop calls. For example, vendors they work with are going to have their own travel programs, which means they likely work with a preferred travel supplier.

Check out press releases. Companies often announce new projects via websites, online newsletters, and press release services. These give insight into possible increased travel in and out of their location (see trigger events below).

Do parking lot checks to see what trucks and company vehicles are in your competitors' parking lots.

Make shop calls to your competitor hotels to find out their rates for specific accounts. For example, if you uncover leads from your parking lot checks, you can then call that hotel posing as a travel manager from that company asking to make a reservation for a future date to see what rate they give you.

Use Google Alerts. As I mentioned above, if you're following a specific industry or company, you may want to set up a Google Alert so that any time a piece of content or web page is indexed in Google under that company name, you'll receive a notification.

Watch for trigger events that affect travel that could be happening inside or outside of an organization:

- Keep up-to-date with financial and investment news and current industry reports. If business is up in an industry, expansion projects take priority. If business is stagnant or down, productivity or cost-saving initiatives jump to the forefront.

- Follow news that could impact government travel, such as weather events—e.g., tornados, hurricanes, wildfires—as well as elections.

- Watch for mergers and acquisitions. Any change of this sort causes organizations to reevaluate all their supplier relationships.

Watch what happens when you do your research and follow the breadcrumbs. Here's an example:

1 You're a sales manager at a full-service hotel and frequently check the parking lots of your competitors for leads.

2 You begin your research on these leads and discover that JKL Maintenance is a company that does maintenance on railway tracks and is based in North Carolina.

3 You make an instant connection. Your hotel is located in the same city as BNSF Railway, one of the largest freight railway networks in the country. The company you've identified could be a vendor bringing crews to the area to do maintenance.

4　You check their website's "About us" or "Corporate" page to find a list of senior executives. You search the company on LinkedIn to find the company page listing employees' names, titles, and how you are connected to them. You look for possible decision-makers with words like "procurement" and "travel manager" in their job description.

5　Next, it's time to do some checking by telephone. You call the local BNSF facility and politely inquire with reception. "I see that one of your vendors, JKL Maintenance, is in town. Are they working on a project for you?" [The desk clerk says yes.] "So, our electrical vendor may be coming to town because one of our lines went down. Who are you working with there?" [Hopefully, the desk clerk gives you the name of the person who sets up the accommodation.]

6　Then you do a shop call with the comp set to see what rates they are paying. "Hi, I'm calling from JKL Maintenance and noticed that some of my buddies are staying at your hotel. I'm bringing in my crew next week and I'm wondering what sort of rate they are getting." [You get a ballpark idea.] "Oh, that's great. And does that include breakfast?"

7　By the time you've finished your research, you have the name of the decision-maker, information about the next project that's going to involve travel (which happens to be close to your hotel), and an idea of the rate being offered at the competition.

Social media tools and social selling

Social selling is when a salesperson uses their social networks (through various social media platforms) to find the right prospects, build credibility, and increase brand awareness through content sharing and engagement.

Social media platforms such as LinkedIn, Facebook, Instagram, and Twitter can be used for one or more of the above activities as you move prospects along the sales cycle. In addition to free services, many platforms have optional paid upgrades that deliver specific sales-related services—for example, LinkedIn Sales Navigator. As these services evolve and change, it's worthwhile to find out how they could work for you.

Although specific social media tools keep evolving, follow these four guiding principles to help you with your sales efforts.

1. Enhance your professional brand

B2B customers want to trust and have confidence in their vendors. You represent both your personal brand and the hotel, brand, or management company you work for. Make sure your social media profile and your posts are aligned with brand qualities that build trust and confidence. A strong professional brand, with a well-presented social media profile and a network of industry and business connections, leads to more inquiries and opportunities for engagement.

Building your brand and your position as a subject matter expert is not about self-promotion. It is about providing insights to your audience that build trust and demonstrate your value and expertise. Are your posts about your company and your product/service, or are you posting content that provides value to your network?

2. Connect with key decision-makers

Identifying decision-makers that meet your established criteria, such as role, function, or industry, has never been easier using platforms such as LinkedIn. And the majority of buyers (76 percent) are ready to have a social media conversation with you.[3] But as you expand your network, you have to be constantly qualifying. Don't accept invites from everybody. It's not about the volume of connections; it's about engaging with contacts who fit with your target audience. Otherwise, your content will not be relevant to your network and you won't be following people who provide valuable content to you.

3. Build a network of trusted relationships

Networking online has similar objectives as traditional in-person networking. You are meeting people in order to have genuine conversations, listen to their needs, and allow them to get to know you. The process takes time because you are building trust and credibility over a series of consistent posts and conversations.

Social media also presents an ideal way to demonstrate your interest to prospects by responding to news they have posted, such as a company milestone, a new product, or a new hire who may be a decision-maker.

4. Engage with insight and relevancy

According to LinkedIn, over 62 percent of B2B buyers respond to salespeople who bring them relevant insights and opportunities. Social media gives you the perfect opportunity to position yourself as a subject matter expert by sharing relevant industry content, commenting on new developments, and sharing content of value to your audience.

Too many salespeople posting on social media think that the purpose is to promote their product, instead of engaging with potential clients and influencers with insight and value. When you share or write a thoughtful post with information that a prospect values, you are demonstrating that you are more than just a salesperson selling a product.

For example, you are a sales manager for a hotel in downtown Chicago and are trying to increase convention business. Think of your audience. It includes meeting and event planners. So, what do meeting planners need in order to do their job better? What is going to help them look good in front of their clients and colleagues and ensure a successful event? Some content ideas could be:

- Top 10 meeting destinations
- Best practices for today's meeting planners
- Planning a meeting on a budget
- Getting your delegates to book the group rate

The key to building a strong content marketing strategy is best described by Ron Tite, founder of the marketing agency Church+State and bestselling author of the book *Think. Do. Say.*, in the 4C content strategy.[4] I adopted this for my own LinkedIn strategy and have seen tremendous growth and engagement with my network.

Consumption: First, what companies are you following? What industry publications you are reading? What podcasts you are listening to?

Curation: As you are consuming content, start thinking about your opinion on the topic. What action do you want your readers to take? What insights do you want to share?

Creation: Create new content that you share in a post, an article, a podcast, or a video.

Connection: Your audience starts interacting with your content by commenting, liking, and sharing—you're connecting with them.

Sales leads are going to come to you from different channels and through many kinds of connections. Twenty years ago, sellers had very few options: a phone, the secretary or gatekeeper, perhaps a website, or a referral scribbled on the back of a business card at a trade show.

The following graphic demonstrates several potential channels and inputs sellers now have to connect with a prospect and learn what is important to them.

**Here's how you might approach researching a potential lead
you know is staying at one of your competitor's hotels:**

LinkedIn: Under the company's LinkedIn page, you
find the names of their travel manager and VP of
sales. You see that you are a second-degree connection
with both contacts and you have shared connections
who could introduce you to them.

Facebook: On the company's Facebook page, you see they
are a proud sponsor of a children's hospital annual fundraiser.
You find the VP on Facebook and see she is a runner, has two
rescue dogs, and volunteers at the local animal shelter.

Twitter: You follow the CEO on Twitter and see her tweets
about their recent acquisition of one of their competitors
and how it's going to create additional jobs across the US.

Website: You see an announcement that the company is
hiring 200 people, with the various job descriptions posted.

Google: You set up a Google Alert to ensure you have
the most up-to-date information on this company.

Take a moment to pat yourself on the back. The
investigating you've been doing is going to provide
you with a lot of information when preparing your call
strategy for this prospect. You will need to synthesize
this information before you pick up the phone or send
an email, but now that you have done some research,
you can start to connect some dots. Everything you do
in this stage helps you have a better conversation with
a prospect. No more smiling, dialing, and hoping that
someone on the other end is going to be open to hearing
from a salesperson with no plan. Now let's see how you
put this research to work for you.

EXECUTING YOUR SALES PLAN
Prospecting with Purpose

"The one thing in life
you can control is effort."
MARK CUBAN[1]

REMEMBER SMILING and dialing Mary from chapter 2? Mary and her general manager were both frustrated because she couldn't land any new business. "I can't get anyone to return my calls or emails." Her performance has improved now that Mary understands the importance of being relevant and how critical research and preparation is.

Yes, Mary is a fictional example, but your results will be real when you are properly prepared. It starts with the research discussed in the last chapter; it then extends to focusing on each and every prospect before picking up the phone or sending that email. It means you'll be able to have a business conversation with your prospect, not a transactional one, as we discussed in chapter 3.

Introducing the call planner

There's a lot of information to keep track of, so when you prepare for your sales appointments and prospecting calls, I recommend using a call planner as your road map to plan out your call strategy. (Download a sample from gillissales.com, in the Resources section—click on Call Planner.)

I don't recommend winging it! I often hear salespeople say, "I've done this a thousand times before and I know what I'm going to say and what questions I'm going to ask. It's all in my head." And then they get shut down by the prospect on the other end of the phone, and the salesperson realizes that it sounded better in their head than it did coming out of their mouth.

A call planner guides you through each step of the prospecting process: What is my objective for this call? What is my opening statement? What questions am I going to ask based on my call objective and what do I know about the company and their needs?

Think of a call planner as your map for navigating the call. It keeps you from going all over the place and ending up with a lot of unanswered questions. And if the customer goes on a tangent, it helps you direct them back to the right place in the sales process.

Use a call planner both when you are prospecting for new business and when you are requalifying an existing account.

Step 1: Synthesize your research

Review what you discovered in your research to identify the game plan for your call:

- What opportunities are available?

- What is going on in their organization that could be driving travel?

- What value do we offer over the competition that they would be interested in hearing about?

- What trigger events have happened over the past few months?

- What projects have they announced that may involve travel?

- Who in your LinkedIn network is following your posts?

Account Name: **Date:**

Client Name: **Title:**

Research and questions to consider:
- Is this an account the hotel is already working with?
- What areas of their business have potential travel needs?
- What could be driving their travel needs? (e.g., hiring, maintenance shutdown, new project)
- Why would they benefit from talking to us right now?
- Who are they currently using as a preferred hotel?
- What do their travelers value in a hotel?
- Why should they work with us vs. the competition?
- Where are we at with the sales prospect? (e.g., you have bid on business before, new contact you have never met, preferred rate in place with no room nights)

Step 2: Set objectives

Next, you need to set your call objectives. The call planner includes a place for this. It's important to understand the difference between the objective for a specific prospecting call and the goal for the overall account.

- Your goal is the ultimate outcome, such as "increase market share" or "steal this business from the competition."

- Your objectives measure milestones along the way. Remember, it takes five to 12 points of interaction to get someone to buy from you. Setting an objective for each call will allow you to be laser focused on where you are in the sales process with this account, so you can get their buy-in and move to the next stage.

For example, based on your research, the objective for the first call to the VP from the previous chapter is:

> To congratulate them on their success and the hiring of 200 employees and to understand how that growth might impact their travel for any new hires coming to HQ for training.

Once you have a clear objective, that drives your opening statement and your qualifying questions. When I am preparing for a call and struggling with my opening statement, it's usually because I either don't have the right objective for the call or it's too vague. Your call objective is the foundation that you build your call strategy on.

Additional examples of call objectives:

- Determine what tour business they have coming into the market.

- Requalify the account to determine potential in the market.

- Determine from reception who the decision-maker is for travel.

- Better understand their decision-making process.

- Gain commitment from the client to come for a site inspection.

- Uncover any new projects they may be working on over the next 12 months.

Objective for Appointment:

Step 3: Prepare your opening statement

Preparing an opening statement sounds easy, but even the most seasoned salesperson struggles putting pen to paper because we don't often write down what is going to come out of our mouths. But consider the alternative if we just wing it. Knowing how difficult it is to get a live body on the phone (remember the stat in chapter 5 from HubSpot that it takes 18 dials to connect with a single buyer), you don't want to risk getting shut down because you weren't prepared when you finally get a buyer on the phone. Consider these best practices.

Keep it under 30 seconds

Remember your call is an interruption and unexpected. You have very little time to capture your prospect's interest. Once you write out your opening statement, practice and iterate before you call to ensure it's relevant and gets to the point.

Never sell in the opening statement

This is the most common mistake. We get so excited that we actually connected with a live body, we jump right into talking about our hotel. "I'm calling from the beautiful ABC Hotel by the airport. We are newly renovated, serve a hot breakfast, and have an industry-recognized cleaning program to ensure the safety of all travelers." You are adding zero value here and they can find all that information on your website.

Understand the filter that a buyer goes through

Return to the sales mindset in chapter 3. This conversation shouldn't be about you; it's about your customer.

According to sales expert, author, and speaker Jill Konrath, when prospects are contacted by a salesperson, there are key determining factors on whether they will listen to or return the call:[2]

- How simple is the request?
- Does it bring value?
- Is it aligned with my objectives? Is it relevant?
- Is it a priority?

Your opening statement must meet these markers to increase the likelihood of the prospect engaging with you.

Step 4: Prepare strategic qualifying questions

This important part of the sales process is, for the most part, poorly executed. When salespeople are having sales conversations, rather than business conversations, it shows up in every stage of the sales process, especially in the qualifying questions we ask. However, when done properly, these questions can help a seller understand what solutions might be a good fit for this client.

They can also identify prospects who aren't a good fit, so you don't waste time trying to put a square peg in a round hole. At our company, we engage with prospects every day who are interested in learning more about our solutions, but not all clients are a fit for our solutions, and we aren't a fit for all clients. Having a strategic qualifying process in place to determine whether there is a mutual fit allows you to make the best recommendations, even if that means turning down the business.

When I started in my first sales role at Hilton, I was 23 and so eager to land my first piece of business. I was working on a big group contract for a pharmaceutical company with a large block of rooms, meeting space, and food and beverage. This was an annual event staying at our competition and I was focused on stealing this business. There were many rounds of negotiations going back and forth with us and the meeting planner. We were successful in getting the contract, but when our director of group services looked at all the concessions we made to get the business, he said, "We should have let the competition keep this one." I was so deflated! I worked so hard to move this piece of business to the hotel, but at what cost? Back then, we did not have sophisticated revenue management systems and forecasting data to do a displacement analysis, which would have likely determined this wasn't a great piece of business after all. It was an important lesson for me to learn early in my career that I will never forget: not all business is good business.

Four categories of qualifying questions

Qualifying Questions	
Business Needs:	Decision-Making:
Competition:	Event Logistics:

To ensure you have the full picture from this prospect in order to shape your recommendations and solutions, build out some strategic questions that fall into the following four categories.

Business needs: These focus on understanding your prospect's business drivers, goals and objectives, and desired outcomes. These are not *your* business needs. For example:

- What are the key objectives for your hotel program next year?

- I see you are opening distribution centers in 10 new markets this year. What impact will that have on your company's travel needs?

Competition: These questions uncover what hotels they are currently working with, what's working and not working, and what other options they are considering. For example:

- What is working well with the preferred hotel you are using in our market?

- Is there anything missing from your current hotel experience?

Decision-making: Understanding the decision-making process, including who is involved and what their budget is, will help you manage the sales process and move it through to the next stage in a timely manner. For example:

- What budget considerations should we keep in mind as we put together our recommendations?

- Describe to me the most important deciding factors in choosing a preferred hotel.

Event logistics: Salespeople usually cover this category pretty well because it covers rates, dates, and space questions. The difference here is you don't lead with them. This process ensures you are elevating the qualifying process and uncovering things in addition to rates, dates, and space. For example:

- Tell me about the overall program for this event.

- Describe the profile of who will be attending.

Developing your qualifying questions

This process develops questions that will give you the best possible outcome. Divide a sheet of paper in half. On the left side, list everything you want to know about this account or opportunity. This is a laundry list in no particular order and can just be your stream of consciousness.

Next, categorize the related questions: that is, label all the decision-making questions, all the event-related questions, and so on.

On the right side, write down how you will phrase these questions. Ensure you have a good mix of open- and closed-ended questions. Salespeople naturally default to closed-ended questions, but one good open-ended question can provide you with much better information.

What do I need to know about this prospect?	How will I ask this to get the information I need?
Are they happy with their current preferred hotel? *Competition question*	**Competition question:** I understand you are currently using XYZ Hotel in our market. What is working well and what is missing?
Is price the only issue that matters for them? *Decision-making question*	**Decision-making question:** What criteria will you use to make your decision?
Are they working with a travel agency? *Decision-making question*	**Decision-making question:** What booking channels are your travelers using to make their reservations?
How many room nights a year do they have in our market? *Event logistics question*	**Event logistics question:** Congratulations on being awarded the construction of the new recreation complex. Tell me more about the project and how many out-of-town subcontractors will require rooms.

This process will also identify if you are missing any questions from one of the four key categories. As you can see in the example above, there are no questions to understand business objectives, so those will need to be developed.

Pulling it all together: Example

Here's an example of how the process will go.

Call objective: Determine if the general contractor will require rooms for the new construction project at the airport.

Opening statement: Hello, it's Tammy from ABC Hotel. I understand you were recently awarded the construction contract for the new hangar at the airport. The purpose of my call is to understand if you will require any rooms for your subcontractors and discuss how we can help you manage that part of your project.

Transition to qualifying questions (don't start selling):

Seller: So, tell me a little bit about the project. When is it going to start?

Prospect: Well, it's delayed until next month and we are behind in putting a lot of details in place.

Seller: That must be frustrating. Are any of your subcontractors from out of town?

Prospect: Most of the crew is local, but we are bringing in two teams from out of town that will need hotel rooms.

Seller: Where are you at in your planning process for finding accommodations for the crew?

Prospect: We haven't actually started yet, as the start dates keep moving.

Seller: It looks like you have a lot of moving parts for this project, and we would love to help. Our hotel is only two miles from the site, and I would be happy to start working on the details for your accommodation requirements. Do you mind if I ask a few questions to better understand your needs?

Qualifying continues, with conversations that "talks" the prospect's language:

- What type of accommodations are you looking for to ensure the hotel is a fit for your crew?

- What are the most important deciding factors when choosing a hotel for this project?

- What kind of budget considerations do we need to keep in mind?

- How many rooms do you require?

Summarize your understanding of their needs: You mentioned your crew is going to be gone for 13 hours a day, and it's important that they have a hot breakfast every morning. Because we specialize in accommodating construction crews, our breakfast starts at 5:30 a.m. so your workers can start their day with a hot meal. And since they will be away from home for at least two weeks, they will appreciate our 24/7 onsite laundry, and our restaurant and lounge after a long day of work. We also have a large parking lot that is well lit and secure for your trucks, which you mentioned was important for the crew.

Based on this information, does this sound like it would accommodate the needs of your crew?

Step 5: Prepare for objections

A sales objection is an expression from a prospect (or a current client) that a barrier exists between the current situation and what needs to be satisfied before buying from you. Once again, the more prepared you are, the better you'll be able to navigate the prospect's concerns and keep moving to the next stage of the sales process. Objections can arise at any stage in the process, although they are most common when a proposal is presented.

Objections in any sales environment tend to fall into one of four categories:

1 Price
2 Lack of trust
3 No immediate need
4 Lack of urgency/not a priority

Here are what some objections might sound like:

· "Send me some information."

· "We already work with xyz Hotel and are very happy."

· "Call me back next quarter."

· "Your rate is too high."

· "We don't have any upcoming needs."

The reason salespeople fear handling objections is they feel they need to have an immediate response and solution. But the best way to overcome an objection is to ask a question. Coming back with a thoughtful question allows the prospect to further elaborate, which helps you to better understand the objection and buys you some time so you can respond appropriately.

The 4A model for objection handling

There are various models for handling objections. Below is one that I have been using for years that is simple and effective.

1 Acknowledge
2 Ask
3 Answer
4 Accept

Here is an example of a salesperson using the 4A model:

Objection: "Your proposal sounds great, but it would be a tough sell to our crew. They have gold level status with your competitor's rewards program, and they are not going to want to give that up."

Acknowledge what the person has said and empathize with their concern.

Salesperson: "I can understand their concern. They work long hours and loyalty points are a real value-add for frequent travelers."

Ask an open-ended question to clarify what their concern is.

Salesperson: "What is it they value most about their gold level status? Is it the points or the upgrades and recognition?"

Client: "It's a bit of both, but I know our guys really appreciate getting upgraded to a bigger room when they are on the road as much as they are."

Answer the objection by presenting an alternative solution.

Salesperson: "We can appreciate that your crew really values the upgrades and recognition. Our loyal guests feel the same way, so we completely understand. We have an option available with our loyalty program that will match the status your crew members have with their current rewards program. They will receive the same recognition and upgrades and not have to start from scratch in building that back up. Would that alleviate your concern?"

Client: "As long as our guys have the same status and rewards, I think I can sell them on switching hotels, especially seeing as your hotel is closer to the site."

Accept the answer.

Salesperson: "That is great to hear. I will be happy to send you a proposal that outlines what we've agreed to."

As you make your calls and follow your call planner, remember that the process is not static. You have to keep focused on your client and the needs of their travelers. Keep defining, refining, and working your strategy. This process is not only for new prospects but for existing clients as well. Sellers should have a cadence in place to connect and requalify existing clients, so you are not taking anything for granted. Use every point of contact along the way to:

- Clarify assumptions

- Validate findings

- Uncover new challenges

- Learn more about the industry and the company

- Develop relationships with other decision-makers in the company

That's why sales is not just a numbers game: it's an art and a science.

Keep going, setting achievable objectives along the way. Remember, business conversations take research, planning, and time. Most of all, they take a lot of listening. When we have a transactional mindset, this way of selling shows up at every stage of the sales process, from the opening statement to the qualifying questions that are asked. Not only is it ineffective, but it also forces the prospect to make a decision based on price because you haven't given them anything else to go on.

KNOWING WHAT GOOD LOOKS LIKE
Hiring, Onboarding, and Retaining Sales Staff

*Hotels have an incredible opportunity
to hit the reset button, handpick the best people,
and build a high-performing team.*

ONSIDER FOR a moment a salesperson or a sales director doing sales for the past 10 years in the hospitality industry. What might they tell you about their experience in sales?

They'd likely talk about how successful they were. During a time of unprecedented growth in the industry, they were able to meet their revenue targets. They grew their accounts by keeping in touch with clients and being personable and available to respond to incoming inquiries. But ask yourself: Do they have the grit and tenacity that comes with making call after call without the instant gratification that comes from hearing "yes"? Were they ever faced with diminishing results and forced to ask, "Where do I look for business outside the hotel's traditional revenue channels?"

In short, did they ever know what it was like to hunt for business in an environment of scarcity when every hotel was fighting for the same business?

Today's sales realities mean that the sales skills that were required 10 years ago to be successful have changed—they are not enough to be successful today. Customers have evolved and the sales profession needs to elevate itself to meet buyers where they are at in the buying process.

Building a sales team and not leaving sales to chance means that your hires have to be effective and skilled at selling regardless of shifts in the market or new competitors, and they need to be able to have a business conversation with an informed buyer.

Organizations have an incredible opportunity to handpick the best people across all disciplines and build a high-performing team that produces exceptional results.

What kind of sales team do you need?

The size and structure of your sales team are determined by a number of factors.

Start by looking at your hotel segment and number of rooms—economy, mid-scale, select service, full service—your brand, size of market, and demand generators in your area. For example, a hotel located in a tier-one market with 500 rooms and 20,000 square feet of meeting space is going to need a different sales structure than an 80-room Holiday Inn Express in a secondary market. If you are an independent hotel with no brand support, you will need to invest in some level of sales support.

And don't expect hunters to be farmers, or vice versa.

Hunters get their energy through pursuing new opportunities. They have a lot of initiative and are not easily discouraged. They are competitive and high achievers.

Farmers are more focused on developing relationships. They are the nurturers who want to provide a high degree of customer service. They enjoy the busy details that come with putting together contracts and banquet event orders (BEOs).

Most salespeople do a bit of both—incoming inquiry management and new business development—but in general, if someone is good at one, they should lean into those strengths. Don't expect a lead catcher (a farmer) to be good at hunting for new business. And if you constrain a hunter to a desk job managing wedding blocks and administrative tasks, they will likely leave as soon as something more interesting comes their way.

One of the pain points I often hear from clients is their frustration with finding and maintaining sales talent. They hire candidates who look good on paper and have experience, or they hire someone with less experience who they feel is coachable. But within six months to a year, the owner is not seeing the results, the sales-person either leaves or is terminated, and the process starts again.

These are symptoms of bigger challenges, and in our industry and in my experience, there are two key areas that need an overhaul if we want to reduce the high turnover:

1   Many hotel owners don't know what they are looking for (i.e., what "good" looks like) because many don't have a sales background and don't know to screen for the right candidate.

2   Too many organizations don't have the sales infra-structure in place to support this role once the salesperson is on board. They assume that if they hire experienced salespeople, they will know what to do.

We'll get to onboarding and training, but let's start with what "good" looks like.

What does "good" look like?

"Good" begins with finding the right set of skills and characteristics for the right role profile.

It's not enough these days to ask traditional ques-tions, such as "What are your strengths?" or "Why did you apply for this job?" Today's candidates (like modern buyers!) are savvy. They know the standard recruitment questions and can adjust their answers to what they think you want to hear. The person they present in the interview may not be the person who shows up on the first day on the job.

Hiring questions for the hospitality industry need to guide the conversation to reveal the factors that set a particular candidate apart from other applicants—in both sales skills and character/fit. The questions should be open-ended and lead the candidate to think on the spot. The idea is to get the candidate to talk openly about their past experiences, so you can pick up any signs as to whether they are going to be good (or a disaster).

Here are some examples of interview questions that have worked for our team when we are recruiting for various sales roles in our organization. Depending on the nature of the role you are hiring for (hunter or farmer), you can choose from the various categories of questions below that best match the role.

New business development (hunter)

- Give me an example of when your research on an account led you to shift business from the competition.

- Tell me about a time when you identified a new project in the market or developed other sources of new business to maximize revenue for your hotel.

- Describe a situation in which you had to use a different approach with a new account because your initial approach failed to win the business.

- Tell me about the prospecting strategies that have worked well for you in the past—and the ones that have not.

- Think of a time when you persuaded a stubborn prospect to switch hotels and give you a chance. What was your approach?

- What percentage of your time is spent managing incoming leads/contracts versus looking for new business?

Relationships/account management and nurturing (farmer/hunter)

- Describe a time when you were able to expand an opportunity or penetrate an account based on relationships you developed.

- How did you leverage the relationships to drive incremental revenue?

- How do you find additional revenue within your existing accounts?

- How do you cultivate prospects and turn them into long-term relationships?

Accountability and measurement (hunter)

- What sales goals were you expected to meet this year?

- How did you monitor your progress toward your goals?

- Talk about a time when you were behind your targets and how you turned things around.

- What is your conversion rate of qualified leads to closed/won business?

Organization and sales pipeline management (farmer/hunter)

- What systems, sales tools, and procedures do you use to organize your work so that you can be efficient?

- Tell me about a time when these tools/procedures worked and a time when they didn't.

- How do you manage your sales pipeline?

- What reports do you use from your CRM to ensure you are effectively managing all stages of the sales pipeline?

- Describe how you plan your day and week to balance all of your sales activities.

Sales skills (farmer/hunter)

- How do you identify whether a prospective client is a fit or not?

- What is the difference between a feature and a benefit? Give an example.

- Tell me about a challenging sales negotiation you were involved in with one of your key customers.

- How do you respond to price objections when negotiating with a client?

- Describe the toughest negotiation you've experienced in which price was the major objection.

- What stage of the sales process do you spend the most time on in order to achieve success?

Drive (hunter)

- Describe how you like to be managed.

- How would your manager rank your competitiveness compared to your peers? Why?

- Tell me about a time when your persistence resulted in a win.

- What do you like about sales?

- What stage of the sales process do you enjoy the most and why? The least?

- On a scale of 1 to 10, how competitive are you?

Confidence (hunter)

- When is your confidence the strongest? The weakest?

- What gets you through a tough day of rejection when cold calling?

- Give an example of when you had to hold your ground with a difficult customer.

- Tell me about your experience with cold calling.

Onboarding and training

Now that you have successfully recruited a skilled and dynamic sales team, you need to develop an onboarding and training program.

Research by Glassdoor reported in 2015 shows that organizations with a strong onboarding process improve new hire retention by 82 percent and productivity by over 70 percent.[1] Onboarding achieves the following:

- Sets up the new hire for success

- Increases employee retention

- Ramps up the salesperson faster, thereby shortening the sales cycle

- Sets up your hotel for success in achieving desired revenue sooner

Gallup supports the findings with its own research, adding that most companies (88 percent) don't do onboarding well.[2] The research also adds that most onboarding is focused on paperwork and processes and lasts a week at most.

The hospitality industry is no exception to this. Onboarding typically focuses on the product and the numbers. In the first week, the new hire is introduced to the product (the hotel and brand), the features (rates, dates, and space), and the hotel's position in the market. The director of sales or the general manager assigns the territory and key accounts, explains how rates are set, and sets a revenue expectation. The new hire gets a tour of the hotel and the competitive set and is back at their desk making prospecting calls.

These are all important things for a new hire to experience; however, it doesn't set them up for long-term success.

Onboarding principles for lasting success

Every hotel is going to structure onboarding and subsequent training differently. The following general principles are recommendations that work for both onboarding and ongoing training and coaching. Training is not a one-time event. It is something that is continuous with opportunities for learning, feedback, and coaching. After each principle, ask yourself, "How might we put this in place at our hotel?"

Introduce the big picture from the beginning. Early in the onboarding process, walk the new hire through the business strategy and sales plan in detail. This will help them see where they fit into the bigger picture in terms of their role, tactics, and overall revenue objectives. When the strategy and plans are reviewed and adjusted throughout the year, they will be in a better position to add their feedback and suggestions.

Do self-assessments. All new hires should participate in a self-assessment process. Self-assessments give the new hire a role in benchmarking where they see their strengths and opportunities for growth. Remember, not all salespeople are going to be great at all aspects of the job. The hiring manager will get a clearer picture as to what additional training may be required. Create an assessment that asks the candidate to rank their experience, confidence level, and skill level (on a scale of 1 to 10) across a number of categories.

Give customized training. No two salespeople are alike, so their training plans shouldn't be the same. Once the assessment is complete, the hiring manager should combine the results with the answers provided during the interview phase. By comparing the two, the sales director or general manager identifies where the new hire requires additional training or coaching. Even a hunter can often be trained to be better at building rapport, and a farmer can sharpen their prospecting skills with the help of a call planner. The result is a *customized training plan* that spends the most time on the areas that need the most development.

When a new member joins our Gillis team, they go through a two-week onboarding program (anyone joining our team has a minimum 10 years of experience in sales). Regardless of their experience, salespeople are not trained in all brands, all systems, and all market segments, and they aren't trained on our sales methodology and standards. So everyone completes the assessment I mentioned above and receives a customized onboarding program where we spend time in the areas they need the most development in. At the end of their two-week onboarding program, our training manager does an evaluation and determines whether they are ready to transition over to one of our sales teams or whether they need additional training.

30, 60, 90 days and beyond

No sales director can wait six months for a new hire to perform. Within the first 30 days, the new hire is assigned accounts to manage, and the clock starts ticking.

Weekly check-ins and coaching, with training as needed, will help ramp up the new hire and allow course correction along the way. The approach is based on the concept that training is more than telling someone "how to do your job"—a concept summarized perfectly in the title of a 2002 sales training book by Harold D. Stolovitch and Erica J. Keeps, *Telling Ain't Training*. We need to show people how to do their job, watch them in action, catch them doing things right, and provide feedback and coaching on the areas they need to continue to develop.

In our sales organization, for example, we often set up an impromptu brown-bag "lunch and learn" to sharpen a skill following a one-on-one sales review. This kind of informal training is far more effective because it takes corrective action right away when a gap is identified.

Long after onboarding is complete, training continues. It is never a one-time event; it is something that your hotel is going to invest in as an ongoing activity to increase the performance and growth of your sales team.

Inspecting, coaching, correcting

Continuous inspecting, coaching, and correcting means you can say goodbye to those annual job reviews. Instead, I recommend the following:

- Performance reviews should be ongoing (as described above) through routine check-ins and 1:1 meetings, which should take place at least twice per month.

- Formal quarterly reviews are tied in with the hotel's incentive program.

This is where the CRM system described in chapter 5 becomes invaluable. The numbers are going to show the sales director or general manager how well opportunities are moving through the sales funnel, and which ones are "stuck" in the funnel. Perhaps the salesperson wasn't prepared enough for the call or isn't connecting with the right decision-makers. The sales director can step in and dig deeper with side-by-side selling, listening to outbound prospecting calls, and attending networking and sales meetings alongside the sales team.

Building engagement

Salespeople want to succeed, and they want to know how they are being measured. If performance isn't clearly defined in terms of expectations, it can undermine confidence on both sides.

Those in positions such as director of sales or general manager need to ensure that the sales team understands what is expected and that their goals are in alignment with the hotel's revenue goals. Be clear about how performance is going to be measured, how often their work is going to be inspected, how feedback is going to be communicated, and what training and support systems are in place to make improvements. This sounds like basic common sense, but I know from seeing what happens in many hotel environments that it's not common practice.

Sales directors also need to understand that salespeople have different motivators. Some are focused on the end goal—a bonus—and don't want to spend time away from achieving their numbers. Others need assurance along the way; they love what they do and feeling successful is part of what drives them. Both need to be measured, coached, and corrected, but the training has to be adapted to the personality.

- Share the pillars of the overall business strategy so they understand how their efforts are directly connected to the overall organizational goals.

- Ask for their input as well as provide them with feedback. This is one of the most effective ways to demonstrate that sales has an equal seat at the table.

- Demonstrate that you have systems and processes to support them.

- Look for ways to celebrate their wins.

- Most importantly, let them know that you value them and their work.

If you are directing or managing sales in the hospitality industry, you have an opportunity to review hiring and retention practices and rebalance what you need in terms of your sales team. But after you've made a hiring decision, there's a lot more work to do in terms of onboarding and training. As a leader, you have to get out of the weeds (doing tasks, focusing on operations) and make time to coach and correct as needed.

You've got your sales team together. Now you need to look at your *extended* sales team—everyone who works at your hotel from the front desk to the housekeeping staff. The final step is to define a culture of sales and service. This isn't something that just "happens." You'll need to set some standard operating procedures to build and maintain such a culture and find ways to get everyone across all departments on board as sales ambassadors. Don't leave your culture to chance. Invest in your people. It will pay off in dividends and will attract the right people to work for you—and bring in the right customers.

EVERYBODY IS IN SALES
Or at Least They Should Be

*"Great companies are built by people who never
stop thinking about ways to improve the business."*

J. WILLARD "BILL" MARRIOTT[1]

WHEN JAMES LAVENSON became president of
the Plaza Hotel in 1972, the famous New York
hotel was unprofitable. He was assigned to take
what was considered a perennial loser and turn it into a
profit-making operation.

After personally assessing the state of sales and
service across all aspects of the hotel's operations,
Lavenson came up with a plan to turn the culture around
within a year. At the heart of his strategy was the concept that "everyone sells." He used an idea of upselling

strawberries with everything from martinis to in-room menus to illustrate how everyone in the hotel could be part of the sales team if they were encouraged and supported. His speech, "Think Strawberries," is now a part of hospitality sales history:

> We started a program with all our guest-contact people using a new secret oath: "Everybody sells!" And we meant everybody—maids, cashiers, waiters, bellmen—the works. We talked to the maids about suggesting room service, to the doormen about mentioning dinner in our restaurants, to cashiers about suggesting return reservations to departing guests. And we talked to waiters about strawberries.[2]

According to Lavenson, employees are some of best advocates you have on your team, but in order to get them on board, you have to start by looking at every individual in every department to make sure they know what they are selling or what could be sold. As employee and customer satisfaction grows, so do revenues. For Lavenson, and the hotel, this is exactly what happened. The Plaza became profitable and remained so each year of his tenure.

The "Think Strawberries" story highlights why sales and service—not transactions—must be embedded in the culture of your hotel. Throughout this book, we've focused on getting new business and growing existing accounts by developing value propositions tailored to the needs of each client. Selling this way is going to attract more clients. But once those travelers start checking in, your employees are the ones who start spreading the word, good or bad, about their experience at your hotel.

Why does culture matter?

Pause for a moment and ask yourself, "What do all hotels have in common?" From an amenity perspective, it's pretty much the same: rooms, beds, Wi-Fi, breakfast, fresh coffee in the lobby, and so on. Culture, on the other hand, makes you memorable and can be a major differentiator.

The advantage comes full circle. When salespeople are articulating the hotel's value proposition with decision-makers, they reap the benefit of culture because those same decision-makers have read the online reviews and already know that you have a better reputation than your comp set. The salesperson has something more to sell than just your rate.

There are additional, related benefits to having a culture of sales and service. Have a look and ask how these apply to your hotel operations.

You have consistency. When there are 50 different versions of what good service looks like, clients don't know what to expect. But once you've developed standard operating procedures (SOPs) for a culture of sales and service, you create consistency. For instance, customers get the impression that everyone at the hotel is happy to see them and ready to assist, not just the doorman or the porter.

You reduce staff turnover. An organization that values culture and invests in its staff communicates to the team how important they are to the success of the organization as a whole (as Lavenson discovered). Employee engagement and retention are high. Staff stay because they are proud of what they are doing and who they work for. They know exactly how they can make a difference each day, and they know it is appreciated by the organization.

Better guest experience means more revenue. We all love getting new clients, but repeat, loyal hotel customers are actually better for the bottom line.[3] Repeat guests spend more money and are more likely to upgrade or respond positively to upselling. They're far more likely to write favorable reviews, give referrals, and in general be ambassadors for your hotel. In addition to higher lifetime value, it actually costs less to retain guests than it does to attract new ones—and during a challenging economy, the costs of attracting new business only increase.

Creating SOPs for customer experience

A culture of sales and service doesn't just happen on its own. It starts with owners, operators, and leaders defining what "good customer experience" looks like for each department, and then creating SOPs for each. They should include both front of the house and heart of the house.

The sops need to be developed with the customer at the center of all interactions. You need to benchmark where you are currently by department, identify the gaps, and create the training plan and sops to elevate the level of service you expect. Refer to the graphic below and use data from your online reviews, brand service scores, and feedback from employees across all departments. (Solicit feedback from your employees!)

Ask:

- Where are the gaps from a customer service and sales point of view?

- Where are you not delivering an exceptional customer service experience? What needs improving?

- What may require more resources (time, staff, training, coaching)?

- What parts are working?

- What does "good" look like for each department?

Once you've identified what "good" looks like and have audited how each department ranks according to these standards, you can create a training plan to bridge any gaps. Refer back to the training recommendations in chapter 7. Training isn't a one-and-done event, and it needs to be far more than directing staff to the online course and saying, "Here you go. Learn it." Training is a process of showing, inspecting, and correcting. Developing your people in this way helps your business become more profitable. It helps your people grow and feel part of something bigger.

In addition to training, those in leadership roles need to model what a culture of sales and service means for them. You are the face of the hotel; everyone is watching you. You have to get out of your office and be seen in the lobby and the restaurant; watch what is happening as guests come and go; be prepared to jump behind the front desk and check in a guest or pick up the phone and take a reservation. You can't expect your team to do anything you are not willing to do yourself. And if a leader's actions and words are not in alignment, people will believe what they see, not what they hear.

Sales is in everyone's job description

Central to Lavenson's belief was the concept that "everybody sells." This has to be at the core of all training and reinforced by those in operations and leadership. Sales needs to be in everyone's job description, not just in the description of the person with "sales" on their business card.

This is particularly important to front-of-the-house jobs such as front desk. Too many front desk associates see their role as "checking people in and checking people out." They need to understand that they have a hybrid role: service and sales because they have an opportunity to qualify guests for future business, sign them up in your rewards program, upgrade them to the executive floor, and so on.

Consider what can happen when a traveler has had a delayed flight or long drive in bad weather. The guest has a hard time finding parking because the hotel is busy. They walk in the rain with their heavy luggage, approach the front desk hoping to have a smooth check-in so they can go to their room, order room service, and get ready for an early morning meeting. Someone behind the desk then asks (without lifting their head), "Are you checking in?" (Not really a very insightful question!) The agent does everything they're supposed to do; they complete the transaction of checking in the guest and off the guest goes to their room. What the agent didn't do was anticipate the guest's needs and ask the guest if they need a wake-up call, if they're hungry and would like some restaurant recommendations, or if they would like help with their luggage. They added no more value than a mobile check-in.

As Seth Godin has said, "The experience people have with your brand is in the hands of the person you pay the least. Act accordingly."[4] This is certainly true in the hospitality industry, where front-line staff can make or break the customer experience.

Match brand values to your culture: Front of the house

How are you preparing your front-line staff to ensure they are empowered and enabled to deliver a memorable experience? The following should be part of all front desk training.

In the service role at the front desk

Front desk service should be more than checking in and checking out.

- Teach staff how to anticipate customer needs right from check-in. For example, "Is there anything you'd like us to set up for you this evening?" or "Do you need directions or a ride to your meeting in the morning?"

- Communicate the policies of the hotel with confidence and clarity so nothing is left to interpretation. For example, do they know the cleaning and social distancing protocols for the hotel and what is being done to keep guests safe?

In the sales role at the front desk

Train them to do sales functions as a regular part of their jobs.

- Be great lead catchers for the sales department when there is an incoming inquiry; learn how to further qualify and close.

- Follow a script and lead form when handling incoming reservations.

- Know your product and your competition and how you differentiate. If they don't know what they are selling against, they will have a difficult time upselling or closing the sale.

- Give key sound bites about the hotel's value proposition. For example, "We're glad you are here for your meeting. Our hotel is known as one of the quietest places to get a good night's sleep when you've got a busy agenda ahead of you."

- Review arrivals reports to see who is checking in without a company name attached.

- Qualify those who've made their reservations through an OTA.

Night audit staff

Don't forget night audit staff. They play a much smaller role in direct customer service, but they can have a valuable role in supporting sales (and knowing they are part of the wider team) by doing more than waiting for a late-night check-in or request.

- Build out a prospecting list from parking lot checks and reader boards.

- "Reverse Google" the comp set for upcoming tournaments, conventions, and so on.

- Shop call the comp set for companies you want to target.

- Research banquet halls, funeral homes, and festivals and get contact information.

- Research companies in your backyard currently not staying with you.

Match brand values: Back of the house

Staff that are considered heart of the house—porters, housekeeping, room service—need to be part of the sales culture delivered through exceptional customer service.

I have a favorite resort that I travel to once a year because of the exceptional service and the culture that the hotel has created. It's unlike anything I have ever experienced. It's the beautiful Hyatt Ziva in Los Cabos, Mexico. I rarely go back to the same resort or destination for personal travel because I like to experience a place that I haven't been to before—that was, until I experienced the Hyatt Ziva. The last trip I took there was a family vacation and there were 20 of us in my extended family group. To this day, my family still talks about their experience. The housekeeping staff spoke mostly Spanish, so the staff greeted each one of us with a warm smile, putting their hand over their heart as they smiled and nodded at us. This happened consistently with everyone we encountered throughout the hotel. Staff had clearly received training in how to make guests feel genuinely welcome, and each one executed their role so well and it was evident they cared. Without a doubt, they understood the importance of their role and saw it modeled around them by colleagues and supervisors.

The brand values of the hotel—respect, humility, care—should be reflected in the way in which *all* staff interact with guests and each other. It's critical that both front-of-house and heart-of-house staff receive the proper training and know their contributions are valued.

Here are a few other examples of what training could include. If language is a barrier with your heart-of-the-house staff, adapt some of these suggestions. Lift your head and smile warmly. A slight nod, or some kind of welcoming gesture is always effective.

- Acknowledge guests in the hallways and elevators: "Hello," "Good evening," "How was your day?" If possible, use their name, "Mr. ——" or "Ms. ——."

- Anticipate needs: "Is there anything else you need in your room?" "I see you are checking out today. Do you need assistance with your luggage?"

Is culture your differentiator?

As mentioned previously, all hotels have beds, breakfast, Wi-Fi, and coffee. The experience and interaction your guests have with your staff can be your differentiator, and guests are willing to pay more for that. Reflect on the questions below and ask yourself what your culture looks like when it's in action.

- How would you describe the culture in your organization?

- How would your employees describe the culture in your organization?

- How do your guests describe the culture based on their experience?

Your answers will give insight into what is working and what is currently missing.

The risk for hotels isn't when things go terribly wrong and the guest has a bad experience. The risk for hotels is losing the customer that you've made no impression on at all. *Indifference* is the risk. The coffee was fine, the bed was comfortable, but there was nothing remarkable about the experience. As chief experience officer Bill Quiseng said so brilliantly, "Nobody raves about average."[5] People only talk about a business when the experience is really exceptional or really bad. Today you get to decide what that experience is going to be.

Being average is not how you build loyalty. You may be delivering a perfectly good experience, but as soon as another hotel opens up in your comp set, your only differentiation is price.

How high do you want to set the bar when it comes to customer experience? What policies and procedures align with this experience? Sales means service and service means sales. Does everyone in your organization understand what this means?

CONCLUSION
Not Leaving
Sales to Chance

*Sales is the lifeblood of all
organizations. No business has
ever succeeded without a sale.*

CAN TELL SHORTLY after stepping into a hotel what
kind of culture they have and whether they are leaving
sales to chance. The front desk staff are greeting travelers with a smile and a few friendly comments, perhaps
finding out why they are in town. Directors or managers
leading the operation are actively involved in inspecting
and supporting those they manage. (You don't have to
guess at this; you see them in the lobby, at the front desk,
walking through the restaurant.) The housekeeping staff
smile politely at guests because they understand the
important role they play.

Dig a little deeper and you'll find that the general
manager goes on sales calls with the sales team and
attends site inspections even though he's always been

a "food and beverage guy"; new hires are being trained and coached each step along the way. They want to improve their results and get better at what they do. Engaged in their work, they stay in their jobs and transition to greater responsibilities. By demonstrating professionalism in their daily roles, they shine a positive light on the hospitality industry and elevate hospitality sales as a respected career.

Most importantly, the customers at the hotel return to tell their travel managers, "There's no other place we'd rather stay." They write positive online reviews about their experience; they recommend the hotel to colleagues, vendors, and partners. They spend more and stay longer. When the hotel salesperson reaches out to their corporate travel manager or meeting planner to inquire about future bookings, the client answers the call or returns the email. They value the partnership and the hospitality provided to their travelers.

Running a hotel with a sales imperative as described above happens when the responsibility for sales and service extends beyond one person or one department. In every sense of the word, sales is an inside job first, and then extends to those on the front lines and those who do it full-time. It has a seat at the same table alongside operations, and everyone in the organization understands they own a piece of it. With standards and processes in place, sales remains proactive and consistent, not reactive and only thought about when there is an economic downturn, an increase in competition, or a pandemic.

If you are struggling because of a crisis, perhaps a slow economy, now is the time to recalibrate. The same principles behind sales as a strategic—not tactical—activity apply even when the economy improves. A sales imperative is not just nice to have, it is a necessity, a *requirement* critical to your success.

Sales is the lifeblood of any organization. No company has ever succeeded without it. Hopefully, you've learned enough from this book to never leave sales to chance again—or, as I like to say, you've learned enough to be dangerous... dangerously effective in building a sales culture that will drive the desired results for your hotel now and into the future.

The hospitality industry is fiercely competitive, it's hard work, and it's not for the faint of heart. But it is also made up of some of the most passionate, dedicated, and resilient people I have ever met. Remember that sales is a marathon, not a sprint. The gains are hugely rewarding for those willing to put in the effort. Let's get selling!

ACKNOWLEDGMENTS

To my remarkable colleagues at Gillis

You inspire me every day, keep me relevant, and show me what good looks like. Words cannot express my gratitude for how you believe in our mission, live our values, and take such good care of each other and our clients.

To my amazing husband

Without your unwavering support, I never would have taken on this endeavor. Thank you for carrying so much of the weight at home this past year and for always being my soft place to land.

To our three children

You are wonderful human beings with so much to look forward to. Find something you love to do and a way to make a living from it. And remember to come home for Sunday dinner.

GLOSSARY

ADR Average daily rate, based on the average revenue earned on an occupied room sold (ADR = room revenue/rooms sold).

Compression Those periods when a hotel or market is nearing full occupancy, presenting revenue management opportunities for hotel operators.

Comp set A selection of competing hotels that you group together when creating your competitive study, based on relevant, specific selection criteria compared to your property such as rate, location, amenities, and brand.

CRM (customer relationship management) A cloud-based technology software solution, like Delphi or Salesforce, for managing all your sales and catering activities and bookings, so you can effectively manage your sales pipeline.

Demand generators The specific economic factors that drive travel to a destination. A city could be an oil and gas market, an agricultural hub, or a leisure destination with beaches or theme parks.

Farmers Salespeople who prefer to get more business out of their existing clients. They are typically associated with account management and catching incoming leads and managing incoming inquiries.

Hunters Salespeople who love to chase new leads and sales. They are typically associated with new business development.

Market segment A group of people who share one or more common characteristics, lumped together for sales and marketing purposes (e.g., corporate, sports, government).

Occupancy Percentage of rooms sold as compared to total available rooms.

Parking lot checks Scoping out what trucks and company vehicles are in your competitors' parking lots as information for future leads.

RevPAR Revenue per available room, a performance metric in the hotel industry that is calculated by dividing a hotel's total guest room revenue by the room count and the number of days in the period being measured.

Sales funnel The way to describe the various stages of the sales cycle, i.e., qualified leads, proposal, closed/won.

Sales objection An expression from a prospect (or a current client) that a barrier exists between the current situation and what needs to be satisfied before buying from you.

Shop calls Phoning your competitors to find out their rates for specific accounts. A ballpark figure can help you better target these clients.

Social selling Leveraging your social network and platforms to find the right prospects, build trusted relationships, and ultimately achieve your sales goals.

Strategy A set of guiding principles that, when communicated and adopted in the organization, generates a desired pattern of decision-making. A sales strategy for a hotel, once adopted, gives clear direction to the organization's sales team to position the hotel and its services to target customers in a meaningful, differentiated way.

Tactics The *how* of carrying out your carefully planned sales actions or activities to meet your objectives.

NOTES

Chapter 1: A Perfect Storm

1 U.S. Travel Association, "Latest Analysis: Coronavirus Impact on Travel 9x Worse Than 9/11," press release, April 20, 2020, ustravel.org/press/latest-analysis-coronavirus-impact-travel-9x-worse-911.

2 Amanda Ferrin, "Why Does the Hospitality Industry Have Such High Turnover?" Joseph David International, February 19, 2020, jdisearch.com/why-does-the-hospitality-industry-have-such-high-turnover.

3 Hospitality Net, "U.S. Hotel RevPAR Forecasted to Flatten in 2020," press release, January 28, 2020, hospitalitynet.org/news/4096733.html.

4 Douglas Quinby, "Hotels vs. the (OTA) World," Phocuswright, May 2017, phocuswright.com/Travel-Research/Research-Updates/2017/Hotels-vs-the-OTA-World.

5 Google, *The ZMOT Handbook: Ways to Win Shoppers at the Zero Moment of Truth* (2012): 11, thinkwithgoogle.com/_qs/documents/705/2012-zmot-handbook_research-studies.pdf.

Chapter 2: Are You Selling Like It's 1990?

1 Brent Adamson, Matthew Dixon, and Nicholas Toman, "The End of Solution Sales," *Harvard Business Review* (July/August 2012), hbr.org/2012/07/the-end-of-solution-sales.

2   Stat cited in Aja Frost, "60 Key Sales Statistics That'll Help You Sell Smarter in 2021," HubSpot, January 8, 2021, blog. hubspot.com/sales/sales-statistics.

3   CSO Insights, *Running Up the Down Escalator: 2017 CSO Insights World-Class Sales Practices Report* (Miller Heiman Group, 2017), 3, pleinairestrategies.com/wp-content/uploads/2017/12/2017-World-Class-Sales-Practices-Summary-Report.pdf.

Chapter 3: Becoming a Modern Seller

1   Dale Carnegie, *How to Win Friends and Influence People* (Pocket Books, 1988; originally published in 1936). See Part III, "How to Win People to Your Way of Thinking."

2   Adrian F. Ward, "The Neuroscience of Everybody's Favorite Topic," *Scientific American*, July 16, 2013, scientificamerican.com/article/the-neuroscience-of-everybody-favorite-topic-themselves.

3   Chris Orlob, "7 Things the Best Sales Calls Have in Common, Based on 25,537 Calls [New Data]," HubSpot, January 4, 2017, blog.hubspot.com/sales/best-sales-calls-25537-calls.

4   CSO Insights, *The Growing Buyer-Seller Gap: Results of the 2018 Buyer Preferences Study* (Miller Heiman Group, 2018), millerheimangroup.com/resources/resource/2018-buyer-preference-study-results.

Chapter 4: Strategy before Tactics

1   Daniel Kahneman, Dan Lovallo, and Olivier Sibony, "A Structured Approach to Strategic Decisions," *MIT Sloan Management Review*, March 4, 2019, sloanreview.mit.edu/article/a-structured-approach-to-strategic-decisions/.

Chapter 5: The Sales Reality

1   Keith Rosen, *Coaching Salespeople into Sales Champions: A Tactical Playbook for Managers and Executives* (John Wiley &

Sons, 2008). See, especially, "Making the Shift from Sales Manager to Executive Sales Coach," in the first chapter.

2   Study results as cited in Aja Frost, "60 Key Sales Statistics That'll Help You Sell Smarter in 2021," HubSpot, January 8, 2021, blog.hubspot.com/sales/sales-statistics.

3   "What Is Social Selling?" LinkedIn Sales Solutions, business.linkedin.com/sales-solutions/social-selling/what-is-social-selling.

4   The original 4C model was created by Todd Lohenry and has since been adapted by Ron Tite.

Chapter 6: Executing Your Sales Plan

1   Tishin Donkersley, "Mark Cuban: Sales Cures All," Tech.co, October 5, 2017, tech.co/news/mark-cuban-startup-sales-cures-2017-10.

2   Jill Konrath, "Email Sales Kit," jillkonrath.com/email-sales-kit.

Chapter 7: Knowing What Good Looks Like

1   Madeline Laurano, "The True Cost of a Bad Hire," Brandon Hall Group, licensed for distribution by Glassdoor, August 2015, bdo.com/getattachment/fc989309-6824-4ad6-9f8d-9ef1138e3d42/the-true-cost-of-a-bad-hire.pdf.aspx?lang=en-US.

2   Gallup, *State of the American Workplace* (2017), 36, gallup.com/workplace/238085/state-american-workplace-report-2017.aspx.

Chapter 8: Everybody Is in Sales

1   As quoted in "J. Willard Marriott: From Root Beer to Riches," *Entrepreneur*, October 10, 2008, entrepreneur.com/article/197668.

2   James Lavenson, "Think Strawberries," *Vital Speeches of the Day* 40 (March 15, 1974): 346-8.

3   Chester Avey, "Why Repeat Hotel Customers Are Better Than New Ones," Hospitality Net, December 7, 2018, hospitalitynet.org/opinion/4091173.html.

4   Seth Godin, "Krulak's Law," *Seth's Blog*, June 13, 2020, seths.blog/2020/06/krulaks-law.

5   Bill Quiseng, "QUI Quotes on Customer Service," 2021, billquiseng.com/qui-quotes-on-customer-service.

ABOUT
THE AUTHOR

TAMMY GILLIS is a recognized thought leader and influencer in the hospitality industry in the areas of sales and sales leadership. She is the founder and CEO of Gillis Sales. Tammy's company disrupted the traditional hotel sales model in 2014 and launched a Dynamic  Sales Solution providing remote sales support for hotels. She works with hotels, brands, and management companies to elevate their sales performance through her speaking and consulting engagements.

Tammy launched her sales career 28 years ago and has led high-performing teams with Hilton Hotels, BlackBerry, and her current team of 35 sales professionals who provide sales support to over 200 hotels across North America.

Tammy has trained thousands of sales professionals, hotel owners, general managers, and front-line associates, earning her a Training Excellence Award from the Institute for Performance and Learning.

gillissales.com

CPSIA information can be obtained
at www.ICGtesting.com
Printed in the USA
BVHW030948160721
611428BV00002B/4